Three Minutes A Day

A Day

Volume 32

Other Christopher Books in Print

Three Minutes A Day

Volume 32

Rev. Thomas J. McSweeney
Director, The Christophers

Stephanie Raha
Editor-in-Chief

Margaret O'Connell
Senior Research Editor

Alison Moran
Promotions Coordinator

Joan Bromfield
Umberto Mignardi
Robert Morris
Jerry O'Neil
Mary Riddle
Monica Yehle-Glick
Contributing Editors

THE CHRISTOPHERS, 12 E. 48th Street, New York, NY 10017

ISBN # 0 - 939055 - 16 - 3

Learn where there is wisdom,
*   where there is strength,*
Where there is understanding,
so that you may at the same time discern
where there is length of days,
*   and life,*
where there is light for the eyes,
*   and peace.*

Baruch 3:14

Introduction

Everybody needs encouragement.

When each day brings its share of problems, a good word makes a difference. Since 1945 The Christophers have offered inspiration to those who are trying their best in a tough world — and to those who have given up trying.

Father James Keller, founder of The Christophers, wanted to help men and women so "entangled in the cares and burdens of daily existence they forget the meaning of life. Encouraging people to set aside even a few minutes a day to pray and meditate on such questions as 'Why am I here? Where did I come from? Where am I going?' could help give countless individuals a perspective of eternity. They will want to do more than just get through each day; they will want to make it count for something."

That was the spark behind the *Three Minutes A Day* books.

It is our mission and joy to present Volume 32 in that series. It has stories designed to give you something to think over, pray about and act on each day of the year.

We hope it will hearten you as you fulfill God's plan to make tomorrow just a little better than today.

The Christophers

All in a name

Naming a newborn is a long and sacred historical tradition. Names endow power. In *Romeo and Juliet,* Romeo asks, "What's in a name?" To Christians, in the name of Jesus is all our hope and redemption as children of God.

New Year's Day was for many years celebrated as the Feast of the Circumcision. Traditionally, a Jewish boy is given his name on this occasion, eight days after his birth. Mary and Joseph, too, brought their son to the temple in Jerusalem on this important day.

Jesus' name — Joshua in Hebrew — means "Savior." Yes, names do carry power and meaning. On the first day of a new year, it would behoove us to honor the sacred Name of Jesus, from whom comes all our strengths and blessings.

"Joseph, son of David, do not be afraid to take Mary as your wife, for the Child conceived in her is from the Holy Spirit. She will bear a Son, and you are to name Him Jesus, for He will save His people from their sins." (Matthew 1:20-21)

Jesus! Name of wondrous love!

Someone may be watching

Almost every day we read or hear about someone who has performed some act of heroism. A life is rescued from a burning auto, an icy pond, or a variety of dangerous situations. The hero acts instantly, efficiently, often while subjected to great personal danger.

In subsequent interviews, the rescuer usually says something like "I didn't do anything special," or "I didn't think about it; I acted on instinct."

These spontaneous reactions to the plight of people in trouble do not just happen. They are the product of a way of thinking — of a mind and heart that have been subtly conditioned to be generous, thoughtful and self-giving. People who perform such heroics have had a lifetime of exposure to parents, family members and friends who behave consistently in loving ways.

We never know who's watching and learning from our behavior. Try to perform a small act of kindness or courtesy toward another person today — no strings attached.

I am among you as one who serves. (Luke 22:27)

Help us to be sensitive to the needs of others, O God, and to be conscious of the fact that our actions speak eloquently.

The measure of success

Teenagers who wear expensive designer running shoes as a status symbol are just following a trend that goes back thousands of years.

In ancient Egypt, people's sandals showed their social rank. Slaves either went barefoot or wore rought sandals of palm leaves. Common people wore thong sandals made of woven papyrus. Only people of higher rank wore ornamental sandals with pointed toes.

Down through the centuries, shoes of various types have been symbols of social rank. So has other clothing.

Indeed, possessions of all kinds have been used to indicate importance and success.

But the true measure of success is not what we wear or own. It's what we do to make the world a better place.

Why do you worry about clothing? Consider the lilies of the field, how they grow; they neither toil nor spin, yet I tell you, even Solomon in all his glory was not clothed like one of these. But if God so clothes the grass of the field . . . will He not much more clothe you . . . ? (Matthew 6:28-30)

Merciful Savior, clothe us with trust in Your providential care.

Young missioner's presence is felt

Kathy Bartek expected to bring something new into the lives of the impoverished people she encountered as a lay missioner in Africa. And she has. But in the process, this young woman is also learning and being enriched by her experiences.

Kathy's two-year stint in the Ivory Coast has taught her that at times her most important role is to listen and "be there" with others. She doesn't have money or material aid to offer. And she can't solve all the terrible problems.

"This type of mission of 'being' rather than 'doing' is challenging me to have confidence in the importance of my presence here, sharing in the lives of others as we connect across cultures," she wrote home.

"In the light of Christianity, I'm trusting my presence here is significant in the unfolding or coming of the kingdom, in the coming together of people reverencing creation in all its uniqueness."

This is His commandment, that we should believe in the name of His Son Jesus Christ and love one another. (1 John 3:23)

Make it possible for us, Jesus, to appreciate the value of our caring presence in the lives of others.

Reach out and help

A pastor in Kansas was organizing an outreach program to demonstrate Christ's love to the community. He phoned several local grocery stores and laundromats for permission to do specific services.

During one call, the employee who answered the phone hesitated, then said, "I'll need to ask the manager, but first, let me make sure I understand: You want to clean up the parking lots, retrieve shopping carts, hold umbrellas for customers, and you don't want anything in return."

"Yes, that's right," said the pastor.

The employee put him on hold. He then came back and said to the pastor, "I'm sorry. We can't let you do that because if we let you do it, we'd have to let everyone else do it, too!"

If only everybody were so kind! Imagine if we had to beg people to *stop* helping each other!

The righteous will shine like the sun in the kingdom of their Father. Let anyone with ears listen! (Matthew 13:43)

Teach us how to help each other, Jesus.

Plant a tree — grow ideas

Nearly a decade ago, 13 eight-year-old girls planted a single sycamore sapling in their hometown of El Segundo, California. "We had used paper plates on a camping trip and wanted to give something back," explained Sabrina Alimahomed, now 17.

Today, that tree is 40 feet tall, and the organization those 13 girls started — Tree Musketeers, a non-profit group run exclusively by young people — has planted thousands of other trees throughout Southern California. Tree Musketeers, which publishes a magazine with 50,000 readers, includes an informal network of adults and young people called Partners for the Planet. And it organizes meetings of young people who are committed to the environment. The group also opened El Segundo's first recycling center.

What has the experience of Tree Musketeers taught 18-year-old member Tara Church? "Don't ever let anyone tell you that you can't change the world," she says.

The Lord God planted a garden in Eden . . . and there He put the man whom He had formed. (Genesis 2:8)

Lord, help me to see the good that can be done for all — and give me the courage to make that difference.

What do you really want to hear?

Want to start a relationship off on the right foot or to improve one that already exists? Try empathy.

Empathy lets people know you're able and willing to see things from their point of view. You can tune into another's state of mind by listening, really listening.

Morey Stettner, author of *The Art of Winning Conversation,* believes that it helps if you follow up your careful listening with a response that let's the speaker feel your affirmation. He recommends saying: "I can appreciate . . ." or "I can identify with . . ." or "I can understand . . ." or "I see that you . . ."

It's common sense to let people know that you understand what they are trying to communicate. It's also a way to let people feel special.

Take the time to listen with your intellect, your imagination, your heart. Empathy is a gift to others that can teach us far more than we know.

Have unity of spirit, sympathy, love for one another, a tender heart, and a humble mind. (1 Peter 3:8)

Let me be willing to really put myself in the other person's place, Jesus, and not just assume that I understand.

Writing with lightening in the dark

There is no denying the emotional and intellectual impact of the media on every aspect of our culture.

There are those who do not trust their own convictions and see in every contradictory image or story a threat which should be removed. There are others who see all human expression as some kind of poetic movement back to God.

On soap operas, situation comedies, adventure films, love stories, whatever, if you look at them through a prism of poetry, you will find unmistakable references to ancient traditional and Christian stories.

Behind the western, for example, there is the eternal struggle between good and evil.

Do not let your heart be troubled if something appears on the surface to run contrary to your beliefs. Behind the action there may be a traditional figure who mirrors some human quality of Christ.

Good will triumph. Our hearts will know the truth.

All things work together for good for those who love God. (Romans 8:28)

Enlighten me so that I will be able to read between the lines, Holy Spirit.

A dream deferred?

In 1891 with professional geographers busy establishing time zones, a young professor, Albrecht Penck, astounded them with his revolutionary proposal to map the entire world.

They enthusiastically agreed and the International Map of the World (IMW) project was born. All countries would contribute. Map landmarks, such as rivers, roads and mountains, would be uniform.

Discussion, debate and disagreement on details lasted decades. Finally, it was time to start making maps and many countries did. But there were always obstacles — including two world wars. Because bureaucratic and political problems proved insurmountable, the nearly finished project died in 1987.

In 1995, Simon Winchester pleaded eloquently for its revival. IMW "created more than 800 . . . of the most eloquent maps ever made. . . . What greater gesture than to bring back from the grave this noble and astonishingly beautiful demonstration of the extent of man's estate?"

Fulfill your own vision.

**Happy are those who persevere.
(Daniel 12:12)**

Lord, help us to persevere despite difficulties and to finally achieve our most important goals.

Getting things done

Enthusiasm is the key to getting things done.
For instance, it was Joshua Lionel Cowen who came up with the idea for the flashlight. But it took someone else's enthusiasm to put it to use.

Cowen made a slender battery and put it in a tube, with a light bulb at one end. It could be stuck into a flower pot to illuminate the plant. But Cowen was busy with other inventions, like his Lionel trains, and had little interest in the flashlight.

Conrad Hubert was so enthusiastic about Cowen's invention that he quit his restaurant business to promote it. Cowen transferred the rights to Hubert. Hubert found a new use for it and manufactured it in 1898 as the first flashlight.

It was Hubert's enthusiasm as much as Cowen's idea that gave us the flashlight. Keep that in mind the next time you get a good idea.

You are the light of the world . . . let your light shine before others, so that they may see your good works and give glory to your Father in heaven. (Matthew 5:14,16)

Inspire us, Jesus, to bring the light of our loving belief in You to each moment of each day.

Are you a lovin' spoonful?

Kayleen J. Reusser wrote in *The Christian Reader* about an experience with her daughter, Lindsay.

Seven-year-old Lindsay was helping her mom set the table. "I'm glad I'm not a fork," she announced. "What's wrong with forks?" asked her mom.

"Forks like to stab things, trying to get everything for themsleves. It's like they say, 'Gimme, gimme' all the time."

Her mom asked her if she preferred knives. "Too bossy," said Lindsay. "Knives always want to change things to fit themselves."

She picked up a spoon. "But spoons are like your friends," she said. "They don't try to change anything. They just seem to say, 'Here, let me help you.'"

Reflecting on her daughter's introspection, Reusser writes, "God wants us to be like that, serving others with a kind spirit.

What utensil would people use to describe you?

Those who are kind reward themselves, but the cruel do themselves harm.
(Proverbs 11:17)

Kind Jesus, remind us that kindness always counts.

A phone call from heaven

In their effort to have children, Mark and Carey Van Druff had spent years trying fertility treatments, but with no luck. They also lost $2,000 in fruitless adoption attempts. Eventually, the couple gave up, resigned to the fact that they would be childless.

Then, one spring day, the telephone rang. A caseworker from an adoption service told the Van Druffs that an anonymous donor wanted to sponsor a foreign adoption for them. Seeing the call as a "sign of God's help," the couple soon welcomed their three-year-old Romanian son.

To this day, the Van Druffs have no idea who their anonymous benefactor was, or how that person knew they desperately wanted a child. But they will never forget the day a telephone call mysteriously, and, the couple believes, providentially changed their lives.

Praise the Lord, O Jerusalem! Praise your God, O Zion! . . . He blesses your children within you. (Psalm 147:12,13)

Show me, Lord, how to help others.

Not too alone for happiness

Rosemarie Schaefer has spent a large part of her retirement on the telephone. And a lot of lonely people are better off because of it.

She runs Happy Voices, a service for shut-ins. When she heard about a network for seniors, she wondered if she could do the same specifically for people who were homebound. Because her daughter is partially paralyzed, Mrs. Schaefer has a special rapport with those who cannot easily get out and about.

She and her husband Frank pay for a toll-free number and some newspaper ads out of their fixed income. "If I can help someone who can't get out and do things, that's what I want to do," says the retired bookkeeper. Despite her own burdens, including the deaths of two sons, she always stresses the positive in her friendly chats.

Rosemarie Schaefer's philosophy is worth remembering and adopting: "Live well. Laugh often. Love much."

Love is patient; love is kind; love is not envious or boastful or arrogant or rude . . . it is not irritable or resentful . . . (1 Corinthians 13:4)

Whenever I think I can't make a difference, Beloved Jesus, remind me that I can.

Dealing with bullies

Why are some children "bullies"? Experts don't have the precise answers but all agree that over-aggressive tendencies can be corrected if parents intervene early, by age 7 or 8. Adult bullies wind up with more arrests for drunk driving, spousal abuse and child abuse, so it's crucial that parents step in and seek help for the situation.

And what if your child is being tormented by a young aggressor? Some strategies to employ include:

■ Providing a "safe haven" home, one where children won't feel like "wimps" for being bullied

■ Teaching your children not to hit back

■ Trying to have your child understand that if no complaint about the bully is made, things will likely get worse.

The sad reality is, there are bullies at all ages of life. Thankfully, they can be dealt with, and their targets can learn how to avoid becoming victims.

The violence of the wicked will sweep them away, because they refuse to do what is just. (Proverbs 21:7)

Lord God, protect us from all who act like bullies.

The kindness of a stranger

Daina Bradley was one of the survivors of the Oklahoma City bombing. To save her life, rescue workers had to amputate her right leg. Sadly, Daina also lost her two small children and her mother in the blast.

Californian Donna Jackson read of Daina's ordeal and wanted to help. She put $100 in a trust fund for Daina and a local newspaper ran a story about her generosity. The fund soon collected $22,000 — enough to cover the cost of a state-of-the-art artificial leg.

The women met in Oklahoma City on Daina's 21st birthday. They've remained close friends ever since. "Daina inspires me to keep going no matter what," says Donna. And Daina returns the compliment: "She always helps me feel better . . . Donna is a woman of great understanding."

The kindness of a stranger led to a beautiful friendship.

Kindness is like a garden of blessings and almsgiving endures forever. (Sirach 40:17)

Lord, make me kind. With myself. With my loved ones. With others. With the Earth and all Creation.

The feline life

Cats can teach some important lessons to humans. Just consider:

Life is for napping and being. Not tearing about madly. Maniacally doing.

Play. Daily. More than once if possible. Find new forms of play.

Keep very clean. And maintain your well-groomed and very clean self all day long no matter what.

Preserve your ability to be excited by the new, the different. Avoid becoming blasé about anything or everything.

And when someone — anyone — does something nice for you . . . purr — or roar — your gratitude.

There are many important life-lessons from your own friendly feline. Or, lacking one or more of these sterling examples of the good life and good behavior, observe their cousins, the lions and tigers at a zoo.

The righteous are as bold as a lion. (Proverbs 28:1)

Alert me to wonders of Creation, of self, of others, of each moment, Creator.

Speaking the same language

Can you guess where these words came from? Moose, Chipmunk. Jaguar. Mahogany. Hominy. Squash. Pecan. Toboggan. Powwow. They're used as English words today thanks to the North American Indians.

Jack Weatherford discusses some Native American influences in his book, *Native Roots: How the Indians Enriched America.*

The first Europeans in North America encountered a world that was in some ways strange to them. They lacked words to describe new sights and experiences; new plants and animals; geography and weather.

One example: *storm* implied simple rain showers but hardly applied to the ferocious disturbances the Caribs called *hurricanes*.

Another: a *powwow* was a holy man who danced. It came to mean a celebration.

Let's celebrate the richness of all languages and traditions.

**To each is given the manifestation of the Spirit for the common good.
(1 Corinthians 12:7)**

Help us, God, to recognize and acknowledge the contributions of all.

Faith, anchor in adversity

Plants and animals can adapt to less than ideal conditions. Trees, for instance, use a variety of techniques to survive.

Douglas fir trees flourish on cold, windy mountain slopes more than 8,000 feet above sea level. They have developed shallow root systems suited to the thin layer of mountain soil. And their slim, tapered tops minimize resistance to strong winds that would topple most trees.

Mangrove trees grow in salt water, which kills most plants. Thick roots anchor them in the silt and raise them above the salt water. And their waxy leaves conserve fresh water.

We, too, can survive in difficult circumstances. Faith in God anchors us firmly. It helps us endure the winds and tides of adversity.

God, who provides for all living things, will give us strength. Turn to God — and hold fast.

Let us hold fast to the confession of our hope without wavering, for He who has promised is faithful. (Hebrews 10:23)

Jesus, increase my hope, my faith, my trust.

Angels wear white

If you ever doubt that one person can make a difference, visit the small town of Bayou La Batre on the Alabama coast. Dr. Regina Benjamin works her miracles there in a clinic she has built to bring medicine and healing to a rural area.

She knew she would need more than knowledge of anatomy to deal with business and government red tape, so she traveled 250 miles twice a week to earn her MBA. She learned of a little-known provision in a 1977 health clinic law that made Federal money available to pay for the operation of a clinic.

Her patients pay her when and how they can. They are as fiercely loyal as she is unassuming and undaunted. "She wants to help people more than she wants to make a bunch of money," said Dale Hammac. "I love that woman."

Dr. Regina Benjamin lights a candle in the dark of poverty and isolation.

Just as you did it to one of the least of these who are members of My family, you did it to Me. (Matthew 25:40)

Lord, speak but the word and my soul shall be healed.

Getting along

Why is it so hard to recognize how much we have in common with others? Why can't people just get along?

It would help if we recognized practices that are common to our many religious traditions.

Compassion. Service. Moral or ethical living.

Fasting and abstinence of various kinds and for various reasons.

Meditation, recollection, mindfulness, living in the present.

Music and song during worship and as worship. The use of sacred symbols.

Pilgrimage. Study of foundational texts and scriptures.

Can we get along? We can if we make the effort to discover how much we have in common. And how little we differ from one another. Ultimately, we are all God's children, all brothers and sisters.

We just have to remember that.

Have we not all one Father? Has not one God created us? (Malachi 2:10)

Father, remind us that all of us have our origin — and our destiny — in You. And that to You we must give an account of how we respected one another.

Telling the 'sweet, intimate story of life'

"All of God's beautiful, sorrowing, struggling, aspiring world."

That's how William Allen White described the contents of *The Emporia Gazette,* the newspaper he edited from 1895 to 1944. True the "big news" about life in Emporia, Kansas, often centered on school lunch menus or farming advice, but, White observed, "we . . . read in their lines the sweet, intimate story of life . . ."

These days, White's granddaughter, Barbara Walker, edits the paper, keeping its contents focused on Emporians' personal experiences.

Local news is also a priority, "our strength and our Godsend," says David Walker, Barbara's husband and the newspaper's publisher.

How long will *The Emporia Gazette* keep rolling off the presses? Well, for at least another generation. When his parents step down, the Walkers' son, Chris — White's great-grandson — will take the helm, continuing to tell life's sweet, intimate story.

He asked you for life; You gave it to him — length of days forever and ever. (Psalm 21:4)

Help me to see You, Lord, in the details of every day.

Dreams and mountains

When 12-year-old mountain climber Merrick Johnson reached the top of Denali, she became the youngest person to climb the highest peak in North America. She carried with her a small piece of rock. A very special rock.

It was given to her by Norman Vaughan, who, at the age of 89, climbed the mountain in Antarctica named for him. He had been a member of Byrd's expedition to Antarctica 65 years earlier. Going back there was the fulfillment of a dream.

When Vaughan gave young Merrick the rock he brought from Antarctica, he was also passing along to her the dream of reaching new heights.

In many ways, an older generation can inspire a younger to strive for greater heights. Encourage young people you know to use their talents, to follow their dreams.

Listen to this dream that I dreamed. (Genesis 37:6)

Inspire my dreams, Jesus. Then help me fulfill them.

Generations of values

Family values. It's a term we hear constantly, one that's been increasingly politicized in our culture. Nevertheless, the real thing endures, as evidenced by Clare Huntington.

In the mid-19th century, Huntington's great-great-great aunt, Abigail Hopper, established the Women's Prison Association, which for most of its history has provided guidance and support for women released from prison. Huntington knows that in these times of shrinking government funds, the Association faces unprecedented dilemmas.

"More than 75 per cent of these women have children," she says, "and when they go to prison the children go to foster care." Even in the best of circumstances, it's hard for these families to reunite.

That's where Huntington and the Association enter the picture. To her, the hope for bringing a mother released from jail back to her children is a victory for family values and second chances.

(Jesus) went down with them and came to Nazareth, and was obedient to them. (Luke 2:51)

Christ Jesus, help me to value and cherish my family.

The price of isolation

Homer and Langley Collyer are known as New York eccentrics who lived and died, isolated, in a city of millions during the first half of the 20th century.

Apparently the brothers allowed no one into their home. And they died without gas, electricity and other modern conveniences. It was, however, filled to the ceilings with packed newspapers, boxes and bucket booby traps.

The bedridden Homer, a lawyer, and his sibling-caretaker Langley, a concert pianist, were found dead in 1947 when someone reported a problem. Police and firemen had a hard time gaining entry because of all the junk blocking the door.

When Langley was found he'd been dead about a month, most likely the victim of one of his booby traps. Homer, who'd been found first, died because there was no one to care for him with his brother gone.

The Collyers are just one example that isolation from others exacts a high price.

For your sake and others', reach out.

The Lord God said, 'It is not good that the man should be alone; I will make him a helper as his partner.' (Genesis 2:18)

Heavenly Father, teach us to trust You so that we will not be afraid to mingle with people.

When life hands you lemons . . .

One morning, Marlee Alex heard her husband announce: "I'm leaving."

Stunned silence followed.

Over the next two years, Marlee Alex fought her way back. Writing in *Aspire* magazine, she recounts the milestones she marked on her journey from crisis — and her thoughts about each step.

● *Own what is real.* "I ruthlessly examined my heart and life for my failure. I asked the Lord to show me and forgive me."

● *Let go of what isn't.* "Take courage because change is tough."

● *Challenge the status quo.* "Pray for a way beyond the old landscape."

● *Open your heart.* "I started listening for God's voice of love in my despair."

● *Put one foot in front of the other.* "It is simple. You just keep going."

● *Don't look back.* "After all, says artist Mary Engelbreit, 'You're not going that way.'"

In the end, "you are glad you hung in there. You are reinventing your life."

Deal courageously, and may the Lord be with the good! (2 Chronicles 19:11)

In my despair, show me Your face, Lord, and grant me Your peace.

You — role model, tutor, coach, guide

Adults often ask: how can we keep today's young people out of trouble? One man in South Carolina has formed an organization to guide youths.

Warren Monroe is the founder of "Boys 'Til Men" in Chester, South Carolina. The organization is made up of adult African-American males who serve as positive role models and mentors for local kids.

Both in a group and in one-on-one sessions, the men motivate and encourage the kids to strive for success. Monroe hopes that by helping these kids, it will provide a brighter future for all involved. "My parents challenged me to dream and set goals for myself," he says. "Many of these kids have lost the ability to dream. We want to give that back to them."

There are plenty of kids in your community who could use you as a positive role model. Use your gifts and talents to tutor, coach, guide them towards a future with possibilities.

**Train children in the right way.
(Proverbs 22:6)**

Child Jesus, help us be positive role models, patient coaches and tutors and sheltering arms to our children.

Emergency landing

When John Mellish made an emergency landing in his plane, he found himself surrounded by armed guards.

Flying solo from Seattle to Delaware, he had encountered dense fog. His fuel got dangerously low and he had to find some place to land.

The spot he chose turned out to be the grounds of a prison. Guards rushed out to his plane because they thought it was part of a break-out scheme.

When the guards learned the facts, they invited Mellish to spend the night in the prison's visitors' center, until he could take off in the morning.

A tragic result of being surrounded by violence is that we become suspicious of other people. We have to exercise reasonable care, but we can't let fear of violence imprison us.

Do not fear, and do not let your heart be faint. (Isaiah 7:4)

Stand by us, Mighty Lord. Please give us Your quiet courage.

There's magic in your hands

Harry Houdini died in 1926, but his fame as one of the greatest escape artists and magicians of all time lives on.

He came from a family that had a constant struggle with poverty. His father, a rabbi of great faith, reassured his family that "God would provide."

One day the cupboards were bare. Ten-year-old Harry took his tricks to the sidewalks of his hometown, Appleton, Wisconsin. People stopped, applauded — and filled his hat with coins. Then he ran home and gave the money to his astonished parents.

So, Houdini discovered a secret: "It's true. God does provide. But it's also true that God helps those who help themselves."

There's a huge difference between trusting God and just waiting for Him to do our work for us. There's no escaping the fact that God depends on us to do our share for ourselves and our world.

The Spirit helps us. (Romans 8:26)

There's work to be done, Holy Spirit. Grant me the stamina and the understanding to do it well, to do it Your way.

A cure for procrastination

Procrastination. Putting off. Delaying. Doing everything but what needs to be done. Ignoring obligations. Making excuses.

Procrastination is common, but curable. Or at least manageable.

● Write lists. Decide what's important. Save procrastination for low priority items.
● Make huge amorphous goals into tiny, concrete jobs. And begin s-l-o-w-l-y.
● Reward yourself with a small treat.
● Build exercise, play and relaxation into your life so your mind will have time to wander.
● Ask a friend to put you on a deadline. And keep you to it come what may.

Not only is there a solution to procrastination, there's a solution to every problem.

A little folding of the hands to rest, and poverty will come upon you like a robber, and want, like an armed warrior. (Proverbs 24:33-34)

Dear God, help me be patient with procrastinators — including myself!

What's the word for "Why in the world?"

Edith Pearlman, a writer, and two of her friends, a city planning consultant and a dentist, recently participated in a community event calculated to challenge even the most astute practitioner of crossword puzzles. In their community, they entered a spelling contest for adults.

For weeks on end they studied the 3,000 possible words on a list supplied and separated into 20 categories including Music, Architecture, Shapes, Weaponry. Each category included a few straightforward words, many difficult ones and at least a dozen impossibilities.

They faced four other competing groups with steely determination and fanatical desire. They missed on "prolusory," having the nature of or serving as a prelude to a game or entertainment. The winning team triumphed on "wirrah," everybody's favorite fish.

They did it for fun. And they learned it was a wonderful way to enjoy a banquet of words.

**A cheerful heart is a good medicine.
(Proverbs 17:22)**

Loving Savior, keep my friends close to me, like the promise to the heart.

A family doctor

The old-fashioned general practitioner, the family doctor, seems a quaint notion in these times of health plans and managed care. Dr. Matthew Warpick, one of the last of the breed, passed away at 95 — yet he served his patients right up until the end, seeing his last one on the day before he died.

An urban version of the country doctor, Dr. Warpick worked six days a week from 6 a.m. to early afternoon in his Harlem office. He often charged his mostly poor and working class clientele only what they thought they could pay.

Even though some considered the neighborhood dangerous, he stayed put. "I've got to take care of the people who have been loyal to me. I can't leave them alone," he said.

His patients taught him the values of honesty, good relations and loyalty, all of which meant more to him than money.

This family doctor set a fine example. Living by our values *is* what counts in the end.

There may come a time when recovery lies in the hands of physicians, for they too pray to the Lord that He grant them success in diagnosis and in healing, for the sake of preserving life. (Sirach 38:13-14)

May I value my fellow sojourners, Lord.

A complaint is answered

As he drove through Mineral Wells, Texas, Jim Rhodes noticed many vacant buildings, due to the shutdown of a local military base. "I always complain to God about things that bother me," says Rhodes. "So I asked Him, 'Why aren't these buildings being used to help the homeless?'"

Days later, a local newspaper reported that one of the buildings was available to any charitable oranization that could put it to good use. Rhodes sent a letter to city officials with his idea, and they offered him the building.

With the help of donated services from plumbers, electricians and painters, Rhodes opened the New Haven Family Center. Since opening, the center has helped over 20 homeless families start a new life. It provides clothes and food, as well as classes which develop skills needed for jobs.

What started as a complaint has become a better life for several families. If something in your area bothers you, turn your complaint into action and make a difference.

Let your light shine before others, so that they may see your good works and give glory to your Father in heaven. (Matthew 5:16)

Holy Spirit, guide us towards helping the helpless.

Litany of clichés

We're living in an age of short hand.

Cliches are ideas gone stale and trite. They seem to proliferate in discourse like, well, rabbits. How often have you heard — or used — these lately?

You have to talk the talk and walk the walk. Get a grip! You don't need to be a rocket scientist. It's not brain surgery! He (she) bought the farm, checked out, cashed in. It's on the tip of my tongue. I'm sending the wrong message? We're on a slippery slope. I'm between a rock and a hard place. No problema! Been there, done that! It doesn't get any better than this! Ya' know?

An overdose of these phrases make you want to run screaming from the room. What was once fresh and catchy has become old and worn out.

Whether in language or other areas of life, try to be fresh and innovative.

Anyone who makes no mistakes in speaking is perfect. (James 3:2)

Lord, help me speak with clarity, wisdom and kindness.

Helping the blind

Today, more than 20 years after the Khmer Rouge reign of terror in Cambodia, death and blindness caused by malnutrition afflicts the villages of this third-world country in epidemic proportions.

Government doctors and aid workers from Helen Keller International, like Dr. Do Seiha and Dr. Yutho Uch, examine the eyes of children, looking for the two most prevalent causes of blindness: Vitamin A deficiency and trachoma, a bacterial infection.

Keith Feldon, a director of the organization, aims to develop the means for villagers to take care of themselves. Says Mr. Feldon: "You have to get things back to functioning the way they were before the war."

Helping people to help themselves, doctors and health care workers carry on with a "can-do" spirit. Hope and optimism are essential for all of us to do our best for those in need.

> **Strengthen the weak hands and make firm the feeble knees. Say to those who are of a fearful heart . . . Here is your God . . . then the eyes of the blind shall be opened. (Isaiah 35:3-4,5)**

Let me not be blind to the plight of others, Lord.

Growing up, growing good

Talk to a child about growing up and they probably think in terms of an age like 18 or 21 or an event like getting a driver's license or going off to college.

But real maturity does not come so easily.

Pope John XXIII offered some thoughts on growing up — within:

"In the world of spiritual endeavor, as in the world of athletic competition, we must learn never to be content with the level we have reached but, with the help of God and with our own determined efforts, we must aim at ever greater heights, at continual improvement, so that we may in the end reach maturity, 'the measure of the stature of the fullness of Christ.'"

Complacency can interfere with the development of talent or ability. Certainly it can stunt a soul. Don't stop trying to be more than you are today. And grow well.

Go to the ant, you lazybones; consider its ways, and be wise. . . . How long will you lie there, O lazybones? When will you rise from your sleep? (Proverbs 6:6,9)

Nourish me, Lord. Nurture me. So I may grow straight and true.

Bless the beasts

You'd think that an avacado-poaching, yard-prowling, spa-soaking 400-pound black bear would incite fear and panic. Instead, homeowners in Monrovia, California, campaigned to save their backyard intruder.

Samson the Bear captured the imagination of animal lovers and the public-at-large. Even Governor Pete Wilson got involved, urging that the California Department of Fish and Game find some alternative to ending Samson's life.

The bear was ultimately captured but not destroyed, and is living in a fish and game facility.

Samson's story serves as a reminder that all life on this planet is precious. We are here for a reason, even the beasts.

The wolf shall live with the lamb, the leopard . . . with the kid, the calf and the lion and the fatling together. . . . The cow and the bear shall graze, their young shall lie down together; and the lion shall eat straw like the ox. (Isaiah 11:6,7)

Help us not forget, Lord, that the animals are as much a part of Your kingdom as we are.

Going for the gold

At the 1996 Summer Olympics in Atlanta, the world cheered for its greatest athletes, many of whom had overcome personal obstacles to get there.

Swimmers from the USA were not favored to win. But they beat the odds and won more swimming medals than any other country.

One of these underdogs was Amy Van Dyken. An asthmatic, she never swims with more than two-thirds of her lung capacity. As a teen, she couldn't walk up a flight of stairs without getting winded. Her high school teammates refused to swim relays with her because she was too slow.

After she won four gold medals, Van Dyken said cheerfully, "Those girls who gave me such a hard time, I want to thank you. Here I am! This is a victory for all the nerds out there."

Amy Van Dyken is a fine example of someone who didn't let negative attitudes affect her. She believed in herself enough to accomplish her dreams. Don't let others stop you — go for the gold!

Do not fear. Only believe. (Luke 8:50)

Provide us with wisdom and courage to realize our dreams, Almighty Father.

Body by Ken and Barbie

For years, youngsters have played with Barbie and Ken dolls. Some parents have worried that they have affected the way children think.

Disturbed by these unrealistic models, Yale psychologist Kelly Brownell did some calculations. She found that to match Barbie's proportions, a woman of normal weight would have to grow two feet taller and lose six inches in the waist. To match Ken's proportions, a man of normal weight would have to grow 20 inches taller and put on 11 inches in the chest.

Brownell points out that trying to change our appearance to fit some impossible ideal leads to certain disappointment and damages self-esteem. It also leads to bulimia and anorexia — self-starvation.

God made each of us unique — in appearance, personality, and talents. We are each beautiful in our own special way.

God said, "Let us make humankind in Our image, according to Our likeness. . . . So God created humankind in His image, in the image of God He created them; male and female He created them. (Genesis 1:26,27)

Thank you for my unique and uniquely wonderful humanity, Creator.

Simple wisdom

Laura Ingalls Wilder is perhaps best known as the author of *Little House on the Prairie*, which became the basis of the much-loved television series. But Wilder had been writing for 20 years before she ever started on that work.

When Stephen Hines of Nashville, Tennessee, discovered that fact, he made a trip to Missouri in search of those early writings. He was on a personal journey as well. Having recently lost his job, Hines felt abandoned by God and worried about providing for his family.

Hines found answers in Wilder's simple wisdom. "It is the simple things of life," she wrote, "that make living worthwhile, the sweet fundamental things such as love and duty, work and rest."

"As I read those words," Hines said, "I could almost feel the presence of this deeply Christian woman. My worries and hurt over losing my job seemed inconsequential now. God was with me, and together we would bring to others this message that so many seemed to have forgotten."

Thus said the Lord God, the Holy One of Israel: In returning and rest you shall be saved; in quietness and in trust shall be your strength. (Isaiah 30:15)

Holy Spirit, send us the gift of Your wisdom.

You gotta have heart

He is known as the "fastest hands in the West." He is also known as an amazing cardiac surgeon with a gift from God in his hands. His name is Dr. Elias S. Hanna.

Hanna, born in Syria, was trained at the Baylor University School of Medicine by Doctors Michael DeBakey and Denton Cooley. In 1969 he was drafted and sent to Vietnam, where he became a chief cardiac and thoracic surgeon. He developed new techniques that could be performed without transfusion.

He operated on Vietnamese children with congenital heart disease without cost. He later set up training programs for Vietnamese doctors.

Today, his nonprofit Hanna Cardiovascular Foundation sends volunteer teams of surgeons to teach the latest techniques to physicians around the world.

He shares his gifts. Indeed, he gives them away.

Immediately aware that power had gone forth from Him, Jesus turned about in the crowd and said, "Who touched My clothes?" (Mark 5:30)

Create in me, O Lord, a heart of compassion.

Dinner with the homeless

Chicago police officer Lisa Nigro was frustrated.

Daily on the streets of the windy city, Lisa encountered the homeless. How could she help them?

One day Lisa and her police officer husband Perry read of a restaurant in Atlanta which fed the homeless. They took a trip and volunteered there, returning to Chicago eager to begin a similar program.

At first, Lisa gave out coffee and doughnuts in poor Chicago neighborhoods. Eventually, she left the police force and she and her husband opened Inspiration Cafe. And just as Lisa had hoped, diners found more than a plate of hot food. They found hope.

Aaron Phipps, recovering from alcohol and drug addiction, says, "Meeting Lisa gave me a new outlook on life. She gives you inspiration to change your life."

Adds Lisa: "If you break bread with someone and treat them as if they're special, they'll find Jesus themselves."

(Jesus) had been made known to them in the breaking of bread. (Luke 24:35)

Lord, show Yourself to us in the bread we share with the poor.

That song sure sounds familiar

E. Yip Harburg is a name you might not recognize, but the world sings his songs. Isidor Hochberg, son of Russian immigrants, was born in New York in 1896.

When he married he changed his name, but never forgot who he was. Like Irving Berlin, another giant among Broadway songwriters, Harburg grew up poor. He made money, but lost it in the crash. "When I lost my possessions, I found my creativity. I gave up the dream of business and went into the business of dreams."

His songs are full of heart. "In a lot of songs I write, I cry. I write with what they call in Yiddish *gederim* — it means the very vitals of your being. I feel everything."

He put his feelings into classics like "Brother, Can You Spare a Dime?" and "Somewhere Over the Rainbow."

Harburg agreed with John Dewey that if you could control the songs of a nation you didn't need to care about its laws.

His upbeat songs also reflected his belief that "If (a song) gives me courage, it'll give others courage."

The Lord is my strength and my might and He has become my salvation. (Exodus 15:1)

Help me bring courage to my dreams, God.

Right? Wrong? And what matters . . .

There are times when we just have to convince the other person that we are right and he or she is absolutely wrong.

These occasions do not have to concern life and death issues. In fact, dig-in-your-heels arguments are often ignited by the tiniest sparks.

Before a few harsh words escalate into angry rebuttals, high-handed attacks, and worse, stop a moment. Does it matter that much? Are the ill-will and bad feelings worth the upset?

Abraham Lincoln understood a great deal about human nature. When a woman wrote him a letter criticizing everything from the way he looked to the state of the nation, he answered her with a note many of us would have trouble writing. He said:

> "Dear Madame:
> You may be right.
> A. Lincoln"

Those with good sense are slow to anger, and it is their glory to overlook an offense. (Proverbs 19:11)

Keep me from confusing appropriate self-esteem with pointless vanity, Spirit of Counsel.

To forgive is to heal

The fire bombing of Dresden, Germany, on the night of February 13, 1945, took a horrible toll. An estimated 35,000 civilians, many of them refugees, were killed. Today the dreadful event still resonates with symbolism for a country that made victims of so many during World War II.

Germans a generation removed from the war and the Holocaust believe it imperative that what took place during those years never be forgotten. President Roman Herzog said, "We want to face up to the past, both where Germans were the perpetrators and where they were the victims."

During a memorial ecumenical service commemorating the 50th anniversary of the destruction of Dresden, victor and vanquished joined in expressions of sorrowful respect and regret. Statesmen, dignitaries and citizens offered prayers to atone for the horror of the Holocaust and the millions who died at Nazi hands. They joined in the words: "Father, forgive us."

We should not forget the past. But with God's help we are not condemned to repeat history, but rather to learn from it and move on.

One who forgives an affront fosters friendship. (Proverbs 17:9)

Father, help us to forgive, as You do each of us.

The promise of a rose garden

It was to be Patrick Cullen's private rose garden but instead it bloomed into something more.

On many occasions, Mr. Cullen had put his talents to work creating rose gardens for friends. Then one of them suggested he make a garden for himself. He agreed with this idea and ordered 100 rosebushes. He fully expected to buy the property on which to plant them.

But Mr. Cullen couldn't find affordable land. So instead, he donated his roses to the Cathedral of St. John the Divine in Manhattan. He also provided the soil and hours of labor. He named the garden the Hope Rosary for his mother.

At last count, there were 400 rosebushes beautifying this urban setting. Somehow, area workers, neighborhood children and others find respite in the midst of city noise and hassles in a place magnificent in its roses.

Behold the beauty of the Lord. (Psalm 17:4)

Thank you, Father, for the exquisite beauty of flowers. Help us to care for, preserve and protect nature.

Great thinkers, bad predictors

People love to make predictions about the future. Their chances of turning out to be correct, even when they are creative thinkers, are unpredictable.

Take William Thomson, Lord Kelvin. The renowned physicist introduced the absolute temperature scale, formulated the second law of thermodynamics and played a part in the successful development of the first Atlantic cable.

Just how good was he as a prognosticator? In 1895, he said that "heavier-than-air flying machines are impossible." Two years later he decided that "radio has no future." And in 1900 he informed fellow scientists that "X-rays are a hoax."

Nobody knows the future. And guesses are just that — guesses. What is important is giving today our best. That way, whatever happens, we will know we have made it a little better than it might have been.

Pursue what makes for peace and for mutual upbuilding. (Romans 14:19)

Holy God, thank You for today. Help me fill it with all the good I can.

The test of time

For most of the decades that followed his 1797 wedding to Louise Catherine Johnson, all that mattered to John Quincy Adams was achieving the highest office in the land. Everyone else, including his wife and their sons, came second.

The couple quarreled often. Still, Louisa Catherine Johnson Adams managed to support her husband in her own way.

Finally, John Quincy Adams, following in his father's footsteps, became the Sixth President of the U.S. in 1825.

But in the last years of the 1820's, Adams found his presidency floundering and vented his frustration on Louisa. He also forced their oldest son, George, to be a lawyer and politician though he was unsuited to those professions.

George committed suicide. For the first time in years, the Adamses reached out to each other and to God for help. It led to a renewed relationship, free of resentments and bitterness.

God *will* heal the past and brighten the future if we ask Him.

Do not judge ... Do not condemn ... Forgive, and you will be forgiven. (Luke 6:37)

Help spouses to neither judge nor condemn each other but rather to forgive, Lord.

Sharing and caring

When Mary Jo Copeland was asked why she spends her time helping the needy, she said: "When I see people in need, I see a mirror of myself." You see, Mrs. Copeland grew up in a poor, abusive home and feels special compassion for others' pain.

She began by handing out food and clothing in a poor section of Minneapolis. In time, her efforts grew into a nonprofit organization called Sharing and Caring Hands. It provides food, clothing, and services to over 5,000 people a week.

Many of the people she helps also become volunteers. In an interview she said, "I tell others to just reach out to one hurting person.

That person might be like a drop in the ocean, but without that drop, the ocean wouldn't be complete."

Send out your bread upon the waters, for after many days you will get it back. (Ecclesiastes 11:1)

Remind me, inspire me, generous Lord, to imitate You.

Time for drug education

In the 1900's, it was common for many of the medicines and remedies to contain high doses of opiates and cocaine. Nobody could "Just say no!" because nobody knew better.

It did not become an issue until Samuel Hopkins Adams began exposing the industry in 1905 in *Collier's Weekly*. Later, because of Upton Sinclair's expose of unsafe food in *The Jungle*, reformers rode a wave of outrage to enact the federal Pure Food and Drug Act in 1906.

Before that, these drugs were legal, common, and pervasive.

Even today the long term effects of many prescription drugs on health and personality remain unknown. Talk to your doctor. Use all medicines with care.

Before you can say "No!" you have to know the facts. God gave us minds. Let's use them to learn for ourselves and to educate others.

Happy those whom You choose and bring near to live in Your courts. (Psalm 65:4)

Become for me, O God, the delight of my life and the joy of my existence.

Gentle strength

Lee Seitz was left paraplegic by polio in 1951. Today, the 65-year-old grandmother operates her wheelchair with her big toes, and sleeps with a respirator to help her breathe.

Even with all these daily challenges, Seitz still finds energy to run the Polio Survivors Foundation. The Foundation benefits people with postpolio syndrome by providing them with motorized carts, wheelchairs, hospital beds, and other equipment.

She founded the program after she had spent 15 years as a shut-in before finding freedom with a motorized wheelchair. She realized she could use her experience to help others in similar situations.

It takes courage to overcome tough situations. Seek the courage within yourself, and use your experiences to help others.

Show by your good life that your works are done with gentleness born of wisdom. (James 3:13)

Holy Spirit, help us live lives which give evidence of Your gentle wisdom.

"Coming along well"

People are amazed that Ronald Cotton is not bitter about the ordeal he endured. He spent 11 years in prison for crimes he didn't commit.

He was finally released when DNA evidence proved him innocent.

But Cotton looks at the positive side of life. He says, "I'm coming along well."

He has a job as a forklift operator for a medical lab company. He's dating a technician he met at work. He's enrolled in a high school equivalency program, and his employer will pay for a college education if he decides to continue his studies.

Cotton says, "I have so much to be thankful for. My life is getting back on track."

Forgiving others lets us put the past behind us and go forward with hope and joy.

Forgive, and you will be forgiven. (Luke 6:37)

Lord, it is especially difficult to forgive those who have hurt us. Help us to pray for them. And enable us someday to forgive them for love of You.

A pat of approval?

Michigan teacher Mary Cooper received an unusual — and inappropriate — compliment from one of her preschool students.

A little boy kept patting Cooper on her rear. She tried a variety of things to make him stop, but nothing worked. Finally, she resorted to a time-out chair.

When the boy's father came to pick him up, Cooper mentioned the problem, hoping to gain some insight. The father explained his son's interest in football — and his curiosity when the players "spanked" each other. "I told my son that they were telling each other what a good job they were doing," he said.

Apparently, the little boy was trying to tell his teacher the same thing. He just hadn't been shown the right way to do it.

When we express appropriate appreciation, we enhance the lives of family, friends, co-workers. And that has a domino effect. Give thanks to someone today.

Give thanks in all circumstances; for this is the will of God in Christ Jesus for you. (1 Thessalonians 5:18)

Help us to be grateful, Divine Father.

Everybody's hero

There is probably no other human being who ever strode off the movie screen and into everyday mythology with as many contradictions as Marion Morrison. He was the paradigm of a good soldier, a compassionate leader, a fearless combatant, and the friend everyone wanted.

When Marion left Winterset, Iowa, to go to California, he was studying to become a lawyer. He moved props and did small walk-on parts in movies. It was not long until he became John Wayne.

Our image of him as some sort of pioneer/western icon was not nearly as close to the real man as everyone thought. Wayne hated horses, was more accustomed to suits and ties than jeans.

For many moviegoers John Wayne was what America needed and what America wanted itself to be. And he remains so even today.

Each one of us can be a hero to someone in real life. We need only give life the best that is in us — and remember to put the other guy first.

God created humankind in His image. (Genesis 1:27)

Give me the strength to live always in Your presence, Lord.

The flowering of courage

It would probably be a hard task to find a person on the face of the earth who does not value courage. It is not an easy virtue. It means facing up to danger — physical, spiritual, or moral.

Anne Morrow Lindbergh offered an unusual perspective in her book *North to the Orient*:

"'The bamboo for prosperity,' a Japanese friend explained to me, 'the pine for long life, the plum for courage.'

"'Why the plum for courage?' I asked, picturing courage as a great oak.

"'Yes, yes,' answered my Japanese friend. 'The plum for courage, because the plum puts forth blossoms while the snow is still on the ground.'"

Next time you must call on your courage, consider the petals of the plum blossom bursting through the bleakness of winter's end.

Surely I know the plans I have for you, says the Lord, plans for your welfare and not for harm, to give you a future with hope. (Jeremiah 29:11)

Enable me to walk into the future with courage, Spirit of God.

Leading teens away from violence

Picture this: an ambulance siren wails. Paramedics burst through the emergency room doors pulling a gurney. The patient is a man bleeding from gunshot wounds. The emergency team hustles, hooking him up to monitors and an IV. Suddenly, the man cries, "Please don't let me die!"

Though it sounds like an average night in any urban emergency room or a scene from a TV drama, this is part of Calling the Shots, an innovative program at St. Paul-Ramsey Medical Center in Minnesota. The program exposes at-risk teens to the aftermath of gun violence, with the hopes of leading them to a better lifestyle.

Before each simulation, the teens are shown basic ER training, given assignments and suited up. They then try to "save" the victim, portrayed by an actor. If a patient "dies," the teens must tell the "family," also played by actors.

"I really cried," said Harvetta, a young participant. "I hurt someone once. Before this program, I might have done it again in a bad situation. Now, I'd walk away."

Pursue peace with everyone. (Hebrews 12:14)

Let us bring peace to all, Jesus, Prince of Peace.

What's that stuff on your forehead?

There is something in us that makes us yearn for some supernatural assurance in our physical world. We still use the ordinary things of our life to indicate and remind us of hidden mysteries. That is why Ash Wednesday continues to mean something special.

At the beginning of Lent, we are marked with them as a reminder of our union with Jesus and His Passion. They also speak of our need to do penance, to prepare ourselves for the central mystery of our faith. Annually, we are brought back to our relationship with God — Father, Son and Holy Spirit. It highlights our human condition.

We are marked as someone who tries to be better, to be good, to be more than we thought we were capable of being. And always, we are reminded of our mortality and of God's plan for our eternity.

Give them a garland instead of ashes, the oil of gladness instead of mourning. (Isaiah 61:3)

Mark me as Yours, O Lord, and forgive my failings.

Lend me your ears

There used to be a time when the only way you could reach out and touch someone was to take up a pen and drop them a note. Correspondence became an art which could be practiced by anyone.

If Vincent Van Gogh had never become a painter, we might still know of him as one of the great nineteenth-century letter writers. He had a voluminous correspondence, mostly to his brother, Theo, who supported him through years of poverty and struggle. We see his torment, his passion, his ability to find metaphor in juxtaposed objects. He also wrote about difficulties with his parents and his obsessive religious piety.

Through Vincent Van Gogh's words we can understand something of the soul of an artist. We can also understand the souls of all men and women through their letters and all their words.

(The Lord) determines the number of the stars; He gives to all of them their names. (Psalm 147:4)

May my every word be a hymn of gratitude to You, God, giver of life and every good thing.

Crying over spilled milk sometimes OK

Barbara Bartocci recalls finding her 87-year-old mother-in-law sitting in her bedroom in the dark, clutching her old driver's license and weeping silently. The older woman had just been turned down for a new license.

Another time, her longtime friend Marianne dropped a jelly glass and shattered it on the kitchen floor. She was very upset. "Ted gave me that glass filled with champagne," Marianne told Barbara, "just after he had proposed and I said yes. It was, well, like a symbol of our love."

At one time or another, each of us has probably thought: "This isn't that important. I'm silly to feel so sad."

But the truth is that our little griefs are real. And significant loss is defined in each individual's heart. Although we shouldn't wallow in self-pity, every so often, as a cartoon caption said, "it is OK to swish our feet a little."

Comfort, O comfort my people, says your God. Speak tenderly to Jerusalem, and cry to her that she has served her term. (Isaiah 40:1-2)

Help us, God, to accept life's little disappointments and sorrows.

Artful gourds

Lots of people collect stamps or coins. But Marvin Johnson of North Carolina collects gourds.

Gourds of every imaginable size, shape, and variety, from all over the world. He has dishes, lamps, musical instruments and toys made of gourds. He has carved and painted gourds that are works of art.

Johnson, now in his eighties, has collected gourds most of his life. To share them with others, he opened a gourd museum, where admission is free. Visitors to the museum enjoy seeing his collection, and he enjoys meeting the visitors. He's made lots of new friends. He even gets phone calls and visitors from other countries.

Why not share your special interests and skills with others? You may make new friends. At the least you'll meet others and enliven your day.

The Lord has ... filled him with divine spirit, with skill, intelligence, and knowledge in every kind of craft. (Exodus 35:30,31)

Thank you, Carpenter from Nazareth, for all my skills.

Running on prayer

Back in 1982, Alberto Salazar had become known as the best marathon runner in the world after winning races in New York City, Boston and Portland, Oregon.

But more than a decade later, Salazar would not cross the finish line alone. God, the athlete would say, helped him win a grueling 50-mile-plus marathon in South Africa.

"I really believe it was a miracle," Salazar says.

In the last 20 miles of that race — a race which lasted 5½ hours — Salazar was so tired he was ready to drop out.

It was then that he began to pray.

In the end, two hours of Rosaries and prayerful meditation got him through.

Salazar now realizes that "the only real success is having a relationship with God."

All of us, too, can find strength by putting our "daily race" in God's hands.

> **Let us run with perseverance the race that is set before us, looking to Jesus the pioneer and perfecter of our faith. (Hebrews 12:1-2)**

> *Lord, help me to always remember that no matter what I face, You are with me, giving me strength.*

By any other name

Ted Geisel was a nice little boy who liked to draw animals the way *he* saw them, not the way they really were.

When he drew an animal with ears that dragged on the floor, his mother told him it was wonderful. In 1916 he won first prize in the *Springfield* (Massachusetts) *Union's* advertising contest. He was 12.

Then a high school art teacher insisted that he draw things the way they are. He quit the class after one day. Ted, you see, had a unique vision. And he went on to develop it at Dartmouth. By graduation Ted Geisel was becoming the famous *Dr. Seuss.* And so the artist and storyteller created the Cat in the Hat, Horton the Elephant, Yertle the Turtle and many others.

Years later Ted Geisel returned to Springfield from his California home for the town's 350th anniversary. Some 600 children had asked for him. After all, Ted Geisel — *Dr. Seuss* — saw the world with their eyes.

See the world with children's eyes! Have fun!

> **'Let the little children come to Me . . . for it is to such as these that the kingdom of heaven belongs.' (Matthew 19:14)**

Holy Spirit, give me the courage to see with the eyes of a child.

A glorious resurrection, a lovely garden

It is a law of nature that a garden needs attention to produce its bounty. The earth needs to be turned and tilled, seeds need to be planted, weeds carefully but assiduously removed. There needs to be balance between water and fertilizer. And then, there needs to be quiet patience and trust.

The season of Lent which comes before the glorious resurrection of the Lord is also a time of cultivation and weeding. For too long a time, perhaps, Lent has been seen as a time of denial, something unpleasant, a time of deprivation. Think of the season as if it were a garden: a time for tending ourselves, taking care to remove those things which make us less than we could be, encouraging the beauty in our natures to flower.

Then, perhaps on Easter Sunday, we can share our bounty with others.

> **Jesus said to (Martha), "I am the resurrection and the life. Those who believe in Me, even though they die, will live, and everyone who lives and believes in Me will never die."
> (John 11:25)**

> *Help me to see growth as I tend Your life in me, Risen Lord.*

The cause of success

Optimism pays off in surprising ways for young people.

Children of immigrants do better in school than children whose parents were born in the United States. A University of Chicago study showed that they make better grades in school and a larger percentage go on to college.

The main reason was found to be "the hopeful attitude of the immigrant parents."

Stressing the need for a positive outlook, author and movie critic Michael Medved says: "The most deadly epidemic menacing our youth today . . . isn't AIDS, or gang violence, or teen pregnancy, but the plague of pessimism that has infected hundreds of millions of young Americans."

Parents can give their children a gift more valuable than anything money can buy. They can pass along to them the gifts of confidence and enthusiasm.

Hope for good things, for lasting joy and mercy. (Sirach 2:9)

Fill parents with confidence in their children's abilities. And show them how to inspire their children.

Domestic animals endangered

When we think about endangered species, we're likely to consider elephants or leopards.

But Kathleen Burke, writing in *Smithsonian* magazine, states that "Legions of domesticated animals across the globe — pigs and cattle, sheep and goats, poultry, horses and ponies — are gravely diminished in number or on the verge of vanishing altogether."

The organization, Rare Breeds International, is devoted to preserving such unique creatures as Britain's Dale ponies and Sicily's Girgentana goat. Though domesticated, these animals often look different than their more familiar cousins. For instance, there is a pig native to Hungary called the Blonde Mangalitza which has hairy fleece similar to sheep.

According to Burke, they "are repositories of genetic diversity and, often, walking textbook studies in adaptation to a particular environment."

In considering global problems, we'd be wise to also look in our own backyards for existing solutions to problems.

God said, 'Let the water bring forth swarms of living creatures and let birds fly above the earth . . . Let the earth bring forth living creatures of every kind.' (Genesis 1:20,24)

God, help us to protect the animal kingdom.

Serving a community

Thirty years of service have led Maryknoll missionary Father Edmund L. Cookston to conclude that, "Rather than the Church liberating the Aymara people of Peru, I believe that we have helped the Aymara liberate themselves."

How did this dedicated man of God bring about a change in the lives of the people in an area the United Nations once called "a permanent disaster area"?

Surely through funding and help from family and friends. But the message he got across to the Aymara was that there was no future in handouts. They had to develop alternative ways to survive. Community is the key.

As Father Cookson puts it, "The overall objective of our parishes is to create a community spirit that people will be able to experience in a concrete, practical way."

Through hard work, this man with a mission has succeeded. So can we.

**Peace be to the whole community.
(Ephesians 6:23)**

Fill us with the spirit of community, Master.

Urban reforestation

When a vandal destroyed the trees in a section of Alley Pond Park, residents of Douglaston, New York, didn't waste time crying over felled oaks.

The president of the Alley Pond volunteers organized a tree planting. Park users, young and old, helped plant 4,000 donated seedlings.

One elderly volunteer said, "People need open spaces."

Her husband added, "This is a place where we can relax with the birds and the trees."

Another person pointed out the benefits of the park's fresh air. A five-year-old volunteer was less analytical. He just likes to come to the park and likes to plant trees "because it's fun."

Instead of becoming discouraged and thinking, "What's the use?" these people took positive steps to restore the beauty of their park.

What problem needs your positive action?

The tree grew great and strong . . . Its foliage was beautiful, its fruit abundant and it provided food for all. The animals of the field found shade under it, the birds of the air nested in its branches. (Daniel 4:11,12)

Inspire, God, our efforts to repair the damage we've caused Your earth, the home You've provided for us and our fellow creatures.

Live the moment

"Full catastrophe" living isn't what you might think. Zorba the Greek, asked if he'd ever been married, replied, "Wife, house, kids, everything . . . the full catastrophe!" Zorba's way of dealing with the stresses, sorrows and joys of life was to celebrate it all, to dance and sing and laugh his way through his days.

Dr. Jon Kabat Zinn of the Stress Reduction and Relaxation Program at the University of Massachusetts has written a book entitled *Full Catastrophe Living*, alluding to the entirety of life experience. Dr. Zinn advocates mindfulness, that is, living in and paying attention to the moment. He teaches that moment-to-moment awareness, achieved through prayer, meditation, yoga and healthful nutrition, can lead us to physical, mental and spiritual peace.

We may not sing and dance our way through life like Zorba. But if we live every minute, hour and day as it comes, chances are we will be able to handle it all — the "full catastrophe."

Do not worry about tomorrow, for tomorrow will bring worries of its own. Today's trouble is enough for today. (Matthew 6:34)

Thank You for the moments of each day, Lord and Friend.

Keeping confidence

When doubts assail you it is hard to regain the confidence that you need to really do your best work. Sometimes you need to remind yourself that you are capable of hitting the mark.

Artist John Sargent once painted a small panel of roses that received a great deal of critical praise. He was offered a high price for it time after time. But he turned them all down.

Whenever Sargent felt discouraged and doubted his talent, he would look at the painting and remind himself, "I painted that."

Because he had evidence of just how good he could be, the artist was encouraged to reach his potential again.

Creativity calls for inspiration — even if it's your own. What have you done that makes you justly proud? What can you do to accomplish something positive today? God gave you His gifts. Use them well.

> **"A man, going on a journey, summoned his slaves and entrusted his property to them; to one he gave five talents, to another two, to another one, to each according to his ability."**
> **(Matthew 25:14-15)**

Please don't let me confuse arrogance with achievement, Lord. Show me how to appreciate my gifts from You.

A bracing solution

Wearing dental braces has long been an ordeal for young people because of the teasing they get. It's humiliating to be called names like "metal mouth."

But some young dental patients have found a way to turn a drawback into an advantage. Instead of trying to conceal the hated braces, they're flaunting them.

There are brilliant colors; red for Valentine's day, for example. Or team colors for sports fans. The result is that instead of being ridiculed, their braces are admired.

These youngsters have the right idea. They concentrated on how to meet a situation head-on instead of wasting time on too much self-pity.

A positive approach can often turn problems into opportunities.

I prayed, and understanding was given me; I called on God, and the spirit of wisdom came to me. (Wisdom of Solomon 7:7)

Holy Wisdom, endow us with that optimism and knowledge that will lead to solutions to our various problems.

Turn peer pressure to peerless pressure

Today's youngsters are more afraid of having no adults around than they are of feeling overly stifled. They need to have the sense that their family and their school are protecting them.

Inviting their friends to your house, creating an atmosphere of respect for attitudes and behavior that may not be to your liking are ongoing tasks.

While associating with other children is very important to the socialization and maturation of a child, it helps if a parent watches a child's interactions. An energetic, creative child can inspire another. Sensitivity grows.

Yet parents need to be alert to any disruptive behavior. They can even encourage alternative behavior just by using their own creative approaches. But obsessive rules will not bend the tree, they will break it.

The constant struggle is finding a balance between your children's friends and the family.

> **Even children make themselves known by their acts, by whether what they do is pure and right. (Proverbs 20:11)**

> *Help children, O Lord, to choose their friends wisely and well.*

Passing through

One of the earliest images of human life in many different cultures and religions is the journey. And with this image, or from it, has come the advice to travel lightly.

Here's a tale from the Hasidim on these intertwined themes: It begins with an American tourist visiting the "renowned Polish rabbi Hofetz Chaim."

And, the tale continues, the tourist "was astonished to see that the rabbi's home was only a simple room filled with books, plus a table and a bench."

So the tourist asked Rabbi Chaim where his furniture was. And Rabbi Chaim turned the question back on him.

In response the American tourist said, "But I'm only passing through."

And Rabbi Chaim said, "So am I."

Life *is* a journey. We are all just passing through. And travelling lightly with unclenched fists and little baggage makes the journey easier.

Remember your Creator . . . before the days of trouble come, and the years draw near when you will say, 'I have no pleasure in them.' (Ecclesiastes 12:1)

Help us to travel lightly during our life's pilgrimage, Holy Spirit.

Neither rain nor snow nor bureaucracy

Did you know that the postal service was not originally set up as a way to keep in touch or get your bills? The earliest organized postal services were set up *exclusively* for government use. It was used to keep nations together, not to write Aunt Millie.

Systems existed in China, Egypt, Assyria, Persia, and Greece. All with far flung and geographically difficult areas. It was not long before it was realized that the public could profit from the system for two major reasons.

First, the postal service provided an excellent source of revenue. Second, the security provided was an aid in controlling communication by the State's enemies.

France began their service in 1464; England in 1635. Numerous governments followed suit. Britain modelled the early American system on the Roman which was itself modeled on the 6th century B.C. Persian postal system.

Communication helps solve problems, spread new ideas and old and unites nations and families.

(Moses) wrote upon the tables the words of the covenant, the ten commandments. (Exodus 34:28)

Stamp my soul with the image of Your face, Lord of the Covenant.

Almost a mining engineer

As a young boy, Walter Cronkite read a magazine called *American Boy*. The famous broadcast journalist spoke in an interview of a series of articles in that magazine about various careers.

"The only two careers that interested me at all were journalism and mining engineering," Cronkite said. "I thought I might be a mining engineer until I flunked physics. I couldn't figure out how a pulley worked."

Thanks to that fact — and one special teacher — Cronkite happily pursued a career in journalism. "Fred Birney taught me journalism in high school," Cronkite recalled. "He captured my imagination immediately. He was also the sponsor of the school paper. He had a great devotion to accuracy and to the truth. Truly, an inspiration for my career."

We all can remember — and give thanks — for the teachers who touched our lives: with their knowledge, their kindness and their example.

Your eyes shall see your Teacher. And . . . your ears shall hear . . . 'This is the way; walk in it.' (Isaiah 30:20-21)

Great Teacher of us all, bless those who strive to bring Your children knowledge and love.

Woodsman, spare that tree!

Albert Korenek has invented a most amazing machine. It's a 200,000-pound apparatus which can pluck a fully grown tree out of the ground, roots and all, and safely replant it. Recently, this amazing contraption moved dozens of old trees — some 200 years old, 3 feet in diameter and 80 feet high — and rearranged them on site. The alternative has always been to clear cut and replace with saplings from a nursery, which have none of the history, charm or shade of a mature tree.

The "tree spade" digs 7 feet into the earth and fits around 38-inch-diameter trunks with petal-like-blades attached to hydraulics. The blades collapse inward and lift the tree out of the ground.

Joyce Kilmer was right, "Only God can make a tree," but, thanks to the ingenuity of one man, we have an option to cutting them down. We can re-locate them.

Do not damage the earth or the sea or the trees. (Revelation 7:3)

Lord, take root in my heart that Your fruits may satisfy my soul — and beautify my world.

A prayer for your talent

Are there days when you feel troubled that you are not using your talents as well as you could?

Doubts about our gifts and the uses we make of them is common to most people. Questioning ourselves can lead to greater understanding. But not if it paralyzes our ability to act, to decide, to create. Our goal should be consistent: to do our best and trust in God.

Samuel Johnson, the 18th century essayist, poet, critic and journalist, is best known for his *Dictionary of the English Language.*

On the day he began the second volume of this pioneering work, he prayed, "O God, who hast hitherto supported me, enable me to proceed in this labor, and in the whole task of my present state; that when I shall render up, at the last day, an account of the talent committed to me, I may receive pardon, for the sake of Jesus Christ. Amen."

Use your gifts. Do your best. Trust God.

Like good stewards of the manifold grace of God, serve one another with whatever gift each of you has received . . . so that God may be glorified in all things through Jesus Christ. (1 Peter 4:10,11)

Thank You, God, for the generous gifts You have given me. Show me how to share them.

Ireland's "hungry fiend"

Ireland's mid-19th century potato famine, the "hungry fiend," was responsible for the eventual worldwide diaspora of millions of Irish people. Through starvation and emigration the country's population was reduced by a third.

The famine also nurtured a simmering hatred for Great Britain. Charles Trevelyan, the British official charged with famine relief, blamed the blight and the famine on "the selfish, perverse and turbulent character" of the Irish. To this day many Irish feel the English government, for political reasons, left them without the resources to battle the blight.

Yet the famine has also been ignored by many Irish citizens out of horror, guilt and shame. But now, the Emerald Isle is acknowledging the defining event of its modern history. As President Mary Robinson says, "Commemoration is a moral act."

Countries, like people, must come to grips with the past before navigating fully the present.

The Lord has brought me in to occupy this land . . . to fulfill the promise that the Lord made on oath to (my) ancestors. (Deuteronomy 9:4,5)

Help us, as a nation, to acknowledge our past, Faithful Lord.

Experiencing genuine satisfaction

Young people have an abundant supply of energy and enthusiasm. Adults can help them direct it into constructive channels.

Nathaniel Shallenberger of Houston began doing volunteer work with his father when he was ten. They helped paint houses for elderly people who couldn't afford to have the work done.

On his first job, working in the heat was uncomfortable. But, said Nathaniel, "The woman who lived there was pretty thankful. She came over and complimented me a lot . . . It made me feel grown up. I did something good instead of playing Nintendo all day."

When families do volunteer work together, children experience the satisfaction of helping others.

Help the poor for the commandment's sake. . . . Lay up your treasure according to the commandments of the Most High, and it will profit you more than gold. (Sirach 29:9,11)

Help families find opportunities to help the needy, Merciful Savior.

Neighsaying at the opera

St. Francis of Assisi had no idea what he started when he preached to the birds, asked a cricket not to interrupt his prayers and tamed the wolf of Gubbio!

This affection and respect for animals can be seen quite regularly on the stage of New York's Metropolitan Opera House under director Franco Zeffirelli.

He puts animals in operas where no animal had gone before. According to Barbara Weir, agent for theater animals, "Zeffirelli puts animals in *everything.*"

In a production of Bizet's opera "Carmen," for example, there were two donkeys, seven placid-to-the-point-of-seeming-bored horses, and three dogs waiting in the wings for their cues.

Zeffirelli says he does it in the spirit of St. Francis of Assisi. That is, with respect, love and delight in their presence.

Make an effort to reconnect with the natural world and all its finned, scaled, furred, and feathered citizens. It's good for soul, mind and body.

Out of the ground the Lord God formed every animal of the field and every bird of the air. (Genesis 2:19)

Thank You for the extraordinary variety of Your Creation, God!

The importance of writing skills

Good writing skills are essential for success in school, work and life in general. Kids don't often realize how important this communications tool can be. Help them by working with them on fun and educational writing projects.

Grab a pen and paper. Try some of these ideas:

■ Have them write a letter to a favorite actor, sports figure, or author. Encourage them to save any letters they receive in response.

■ Keep a travel diary on vacation noting places visited and points of interest. Add photos for a real keepsake.

■ Help them write a persuasive "letter to the editor" about an issue that concerns them.

■ Show kids how to write thank you notes for gifts and favors.

■ Have fun writing a television or movie script. This also encourages creativity.

A child who learns good communication skills today will be an excellent leader tomorrow.

> **Those who are wise shall shine like the brightness of the sky, and those who lead the many to righteousness, like the stars. (Daniel 12:3)**

> *Show us how to lead children to a successful future, Holy Spirit.*

Cultivating hope, one weed at a time

If you find yourself discouraged when your best efforts are slow-going, meet Fredrika Lightfoot.

She lives with her mother on Chicago's South Side. It's an area where elderly people live uneasily side-by-side with drug addicts. Violence and poverty vie with apathy and fear as obstacles to a decent neighborhood. But Fredrika Lightfoot dreams of beautiful, safe oases.

More than just dream about them, she has created them. Within a couple of years she cleared six lots of debris and weeds. She planted simple gardens using old tires as planters and painted rubble as borders for flower beds.

These green spaces are respected. One crack house was scheduled for demolition, but with a garden blooming next door, the city renovated the building. A family has moved in.

Now neighbors are involved. And Fredrika Lightfoot just keeps going. "I tell myself, 'I'll get those ten weeds today, and those three tomorrow.' That gives me a goal, so I don't get discouraged."

Simple goals leave no room for the weeds of discouragement.

I have put my hope in the Everlasting. (Baruch 4:22)

Nurture in me, Lord, seeds of hope that I can sow for others.

Village of hope

About half the people in Camphill Village in Upstate New York are "challenged" — either mentally or physically. The other half are called "co-workers": people who raise their families in homes they share with the "challenged" and share the farming and other work of the village with them as well.

"We're not thinking, 'What can we do to help them?'" said Deborah Admiral, a co-worker. "We think, 'How can we help them to find their particular gifts and make a contribution to our common life?'"

Said Ellen Roberts, who grew up in the village, "I've enjoyed the feeling of helping people when they need me and having people there to help me."

Each of us has special gifts and talents which can benefit all of us: in a home or on a job. We need to look around to find out what these gifts are.

**To each is given the manifestation of the Spirit for the common good.
(1 Corinthians 12:7)**

Savior, show me how I can help others — and how they can help me.

Career advancement

LaVonne Neal had it all: a high-powered corporate job, a townhouse, annual vacations in Europe. But something was missing.

In her reflective moments, she remembered how important a teacher had been to her in middle school. "She saw something in me, pulled me aside, and taught me how to channel my talents. She gave me the direction I needed at a critical point in my life."

When LaVonne Neal could not take the emptiness any longer she quit her job and went back to school to become a teacher. She earned her credentials in a year and landed a job at Grisham Middle School in Round Rock, Texas. Gone is the luxury, the European vacations. Instead, she puts in long hours, continues to go to school for her master of education degree, and earns nearly half of what she once earned.

But she is laying up treasure by sharing her real wealth. And feeling good about herself.

The souls of the righteous . . . will shine forth, and will run like sparks through the stubble. (Wisdom 3:1,7)

Put more love in my heart, Lord of Love, that, like You, I might give it away.

A grandmother's legacy

Imagine being 17 again. Imagine inheriting $20,000 at the age of 17. What would you do with the money? Buy a car, perhaps, pay for college, or maybe even celebrate with a party and some new clothes? Or would you use it to help others?

Gillian Kilberg, a 17-year-old from McLean, Virginia, inherited $20,000 when her grandmother died. She chose to use the money to honor her grandmother's memory and opened a day camp for needy children called Grandma Rita's Children. These kids get to experience things they might never have before, such as baseball games and concerts.

"This lets these kids be kids and gives them hope that there is a world outside their everyday environment," said Gillian.

Any grandmother would be proud of such a kind and unselfish grandchild. What legacy will you leave for the next generation?

I know the plans I have for you, says the Lord, plans for your welfare and not for harm, to give you a future with hope. (Jeremiah 29:11)

Almighty Father, remind us to provide hope for those who will follow us.

Obligation to yourself

While human beings have always had to struggle with morality, it's hard to grasp the growing amorality that some see as the norm.

Barbara Tuchman, the Pulitzer Prize-winning author and historian has described our times as "The Age of Disruption, a period when we've lost belief in certain kinds of moral understanding of good and bad."

What do we need as we face the next century? "Probably personal responsibility," according to Tuchman. "Taking responsibility for your behavior and your expenditures and your actions, and not forever supposing that society must forgive you because it's not your fault."

How often have we heard, "It's not my fault"? How often have we said it ourselves? It makes no sense to take responsibility or to feel guilty about every bad thing.

But just maybe, a higher standard of morality and a greater sense of obligation is in order.

**Graciously teach me Your law.
(Psalm 119:29)**

Holy Lord, guide me not only as I examine my conscience, but as I try to develop it in accordance with Your Will.

Acknowledging the source of our talents

How does a star athlete keep self-confidence from becoming arrogance and conceit?

It's not a problem just for superstars. To some extent all people face it. Coach Leslie Frazier, a former NFL star, has this to say:

"There's nothing wrong with confidence. I believe it's impossible to be a great athlete without it . . . But always remember the reason you're good. Thank God for your athletic talent. You're a good athlete not because of what you do in the weight room or how fast you run, or how high you jump. It's only by the grace of God that you have those abilities."

As Frazier reminds us, self-confidence means recognizing our special abilities.

Arrogance comes when we don't recognize that they're a gift of God.

The Lord's gift remains with the devout, and His favor brings lasting success.
(Sirach 11:17)

Lord God, thank You for Your many gifts.

Philanthropist washes clothes for a living

Oseola McCarty, 88, of Hattiesburg, Mississippi, astonished many when she gave $150,000 to the University of Southern Mississippi "to help African-American children who are eager for learning like I was, but whose families can't afford to send them to school."

It's not unheard of for a person of means who has worked a lifetime to set up a scholarship fund. Ms. McCarty had herself enjoyed school, though she left in sixth grade to care for an ailing relative. But what was surprising was that her life's work had been washing and ironing clothes.

Ms. McCarty loved her work and did it well. She also saved wisely. The first scholarship recipient is like a granddaughter, she says. When people ask why she didn't use the money for herself, she replies, "Thanks to the good Lord I *am* spending it on myself."

Indeed, by helping others you do help yourself.

A generous person will be enriched. (Proverbs 11:25)

Guide us in Your generous ways, Lord.

A rare breed

Susanna Davy is the shepherd of a flock of rare and endangered sheep.

America used to be rich with a wide variety of breeds, but now there are only a few standardized, specialized breeds. Ms. Davy cares for 150 to 200 sheep which includes five minor or rare breeds: St. Croix, Barbados, Cotswold, Karakul and Jacob sheep. "The minor breeds of livestock are facing extinction. We can't let this happen."

Don't think that being a shepherd is some idyllic time in a pasture, playing a flute and watching the clouds. The job involves a great deal of work: lambing, tending miles of electric fence, cleaning the barn, keeping meticulous breeding, birth and death records, shearing, rabies shots, trimming hoofs and watching out for coyotes.

Hard work, but when you see Susanna Davy holding one of her small black and white Jacob lambs, you know she wouldn't change jobs for the world.

I myself will be the shepherd of My sheep . . . I will seek the lost, and I will bring back the strayed, and I will bind up the injured, and I will strengthen the weak. (Ezekiel 34:15,16)

When I am lost, O Lord, find me, put me on Your shoulders.

Boosting literacy

"I thought an interesting thing to do would be to go where poets don't go," said U.S. Poet Laureate Robert Hass. "The thing to talk about is not poetic 'uplift,' but the fact that basic literacy in this country is in a serious crisis."

And so the celebrated poet became an activist, leaving the literary cocoon behind and spending much of the last two years traveling to and speaking at business and civic gatherings, sounding the alarm that literary standards have nosedived. He's been asking community leaders what they intend to do to insure that their children will read poems and stories.

"Did it do any good?" Hass wonders. "It's like teaching. You have no idea."

Nothing ventured, nothing gained. Robert Hass not only talks the talk, he walks the walk.

We are all judged by our actions.

Great as His mercy, so also is His chastisement; He judges a person according to one's deeds. (Sirach 16:12)

Father, instill in me the desire to take action.

Second chances

For Mary West, life has been a series of second chances.

As a young girl growing up in New Hampshire, West and her 11 siblings faced her father's illness. Help and hope came from the Salvation Army.

In her 20s, West herself joined the Salvation Army, but her time with the group was short. She "dropped out" of the Army and society, began abusing drugs and alcohol, and eventually found herself pregnant and alone.

Then, West had a vision. "I saw Jesus and heard Him," she says. She cleaned up her act, and got her life back on track, raising her son and working.

These days West is once again part of the Salvation Army. She decided to give the group who preaches the "Gospel of the Second Chance" one of its own.

West says that a lot of people have "put hope back in my life," and how she wants to offer others that same hope — and second chance.

> **Blessed are those who trust in the Lord . . . They shall be like a tree planted by water, sending out its roots by the stream. (Jeremiah 17:7,8)**

> *Master, You alone are our source of hope and our consolation.*

But, what do YOU think?

One lesson Connecticut Congressman Gary Franks learned in college was not written in any textbook.

"I remember taking copious notes and listening to everything the teacher had to say in preparation for my first test at Yale," Franks said. "I looked at the exam and saw it was everything I had studied. I wrote the answers to the three questions thinking, 'Boy, this is easy.'"

Then he got the test back. The grade — an easy "A," Franks had thought — was a "C." Written under the grade was this message from the teacher: "I know what I said: What do you think?"

That incident taught Franks to not simply absorb ideas but "to think about them and challenge them." Franks observes: "It forced me to explore things from every possible angle, looking for aspects that might not be obvious at first but were helpful in developing a dialogue on an issue."

Don't be afraid to think, to question, to explore. You have the God-given ability to do so.

The Lord created human beings out of the earth . . . Discretion and tongue and eyes, ears and a mind for thinking He gave them. (Sirach 17:1,6)

Creator, open my heart and my mind to all You make possible.

The clown and the parking meters

In Santa Cruz, California, a clown named "Mr. Twister" was chased down a street by a meter reader who spotted him slipping coins into a stranger's parking meter.

Police wrote the man in the clown suit a ticket for "unauthorized deposit of coins" in parking meters. But that won't stop Mr. Twister.

"No matter what they do to me," he says, "I'm never going to stop." In fact, Mr. Twister says that people have begun to give him coins and encourage him to keep feeding meters.

Although we may not have to go so far as to dress in a clown suit, each of us every day can find a way to reach out to others through an act of kindness.

Do not neglect to do good. (Hebrews 13:16)

Lord, help us to see the opportunities You show us every day to bring Your light and love into the lives of others.

A vision in stone

Seeing the possibility in any circumstance is the first step in turning it into reality.

Around the year 1500, a sculptor named Simone da Fiesole chose a huge block of fine marble for a larger-than-life figure. His patrons were quickly appalled by his crude carving and stopped the project.

Another artist had seen the marble. And in spite of the damage, he still believed it contained the possibility for something extraordinary. It took three years for the sculptor's imagination, energy and talent to transform the stone. In 1504, the statue was unveiled in Florence's Piazza della Signoria. For the first time the world marveled at Michelangelo's *David*.

Michelangelo had a gift that allowed him to create with his hands the beauty he saw with his mind. Five hundred years later it still enriches others.

Even if your gifts seem less spectacular, use them to reflect what is good and true. Recognize possibilities — and roll up your sleeves.

I was naturally gifted. (Wisdom 8:19)

You have given me gifts, Holy God, to use as well, as completely, as beautifully as I can. Grant me the vision and the will to serve.

Christmas in April

For some people, Santa Claus arrives in early spring. He exchanges his red suit and sleigh for a hammer and nails and rather than sliding down the chimney, he's busy fixing it.

These industrious Santas are members of Christmas in April, a national volunteer organization that helps low income homeowners fix their houses. If the owners meet federal poverty guidelines and organizational criteria, 20 to 25 volunteers launch a one day mission of repair.

The program is the joint effort of private citizens and corporate sponsors. While volunteers perform all the actual repairs, local building-supply companies provide the materials and nearby restaurants provide workers with food. Houses that were unsafe and in disrepair are transformed into welcoming homes, but the real achievements are the bonds that form when neighbors work together for a common cause.

Money is not always the answer. We can give of our hearts, heads, and hands too. Donate your time and talents graciously to those in need.

Some give freely, yet grow all the richer; others withhold what is due, and only suffer want. A generous person will be enriched. (Proverbs 11:24-25)

Carpenter of Nazareth, teach me to build with the gifts You have given me.

Six steps to making effective resolutions

Decide what is important to you and plan to change 24 hours at a time. If you are making a resolution for any reason other than what you want or need, you are courting failure.

Don't make exhaustive lists. If you over-think or over-plan it, it could seem impossible.

Don't look too far ahead. Deal with the here and now. Take simple steps to get to your goal each day.

Surround yourself with positive people. People who don't want the best for you are not worthy of you.

Be kind to yourself. Deadlines can cause a lot of stress. Be firm, but be gentle with yourself.

Congratulate yourself for trying daily. The impulse to change and the courage to continue is not to be taken lightly.

Determination and persistence build strength and that leads to success.

Forgetting what lies behind and straining forward to what lies ahead, I press on toward the goal. (Philippians 3:13-14)

Give me the patience to succeed, and the understanding to fail.

Sowing the seeds of prayer

It started with a simple experiment for the children of Guttenburg United Methodist Church in Guttenburg, Iowa. The pastor took two pie tins and filled them with soil and seeds. One tin was prayed over, the other was not.

After a few weeks and some doubts from parishioners, the blessed seeds grew better than the unblessed seeds. Pastor Karl Goodfellow, who conducted the experiment, said, "After the results I think everyone felt it worked just the way prayer is supposed to work."

This simple demonstration blossomed into the Safety Net Prayer Chain, enthusiastic intercessors who pray for the lives of 100,000 Iowa farmers during the harvest season. Launched from the Guttenburg church, it has since grown to include other churches and groups statewide.

People involved in the prayer chain have shared stories of how their prayers have worked; Goodfellow's own nephew miraculously survived a farming accident.

The power of prayer. Try it for yourself.

Whatever you ask for in prayer with faith, you will receive. (Matthew 21:22)

Lord, help me pray to You with a faithful heart.

Carving out a special niche

The Royal Family of Spain has one. The Pope has one. You can have one, too, if you travel the highway to Tobati, Paraguay, and the workshop-home of Don Zenon Paez Esquivel.

Don Paez is one of the masters of the *santeros*, or saint makers. Don Paez carves images of saints from cedar. He keeps the iconography of over 100 saints in memory: which *santeros* needs a dog (Saint Rock), a plow (Saint Isadore), or a monstrance for the Eucharist (Saint Clare). When in doubt, he consults his large collection of holy cards or the parish priest.

Many of the Paez clan have also turned to carving. Some use near assembly line techniques. Others, like Don Zenon Paez, take days just to carve each statue. Getulio Paez says the statues "should have a convincing human appearance."

It's important to work at a human pace so that what we produce gives evidence of our humanity.

> **God said, "Let Us make humankind in Our image, according to Our likeness."**
> **(Genesis 1:26)**

> *Carpenter of Nazareth, may the work of my hands help sanctify me.*

When the weather is stormy . . .

Every one of us has faced bad times. Writer Diane J. Moore offers the following guidelines to empower and inspire you:

● *Develop patience.* "Never think that God's delays are God's denials," wrote French naturalist Georges Louis Buffon.

● *Forget luck.* Moore's mother once said: "If you don't put feet on those prayers, nothing will happen."

● *Don't sabotage yourself.* Look at yourself as an observer, not a critic.

● *Never give somebody's opinion more importance than your own.* "No one," Eleanor Roosevelt said, "can make you feel inferior without your consent."

● *Learn from children.* Live for today.

● *Forget age.* Life is an opportunity to make a difference each and every day.

● *Accept yourself as you are.* Believe in yourself, as God does. The world will be brighter for everyone.

Take delight in the Lord . . . Commit your way to the Lord; trust in Him and He will act. (Psalm 37:4,5)

Lord, in our darkest moments, help us to remember that Easter Sunday followed Good Friday.

The power to forgive

John Perkins knows how tough it can be to forgive others when they hurt us. But he's made forgiveness his life's work.

Perkins works with Voice of Calvary Ministries and the Foundation for Reconciliation and Development to break down racial injustices. An event that happened nearly 30 years ago prepared him for his work.

"In 1970, I was almost beaten to death by the police in the Brandon, Mississippi, jail," says Perkins. "That night I made a promise to God that if He would allow me to come out of jail alive, I would be true to preaching the Gospel. But I had to go through a period of trying to forgive the sheriff and policemen who had brutalized me; I knew I needed to forgive white people to be able to trust them in the future. I was broken in that jail. Then came my healing."

When your heart is broken, pray to God for healing and the power to forgive.

**Forgive, and you will be forgiven.
(Luke 6:37)**

Enable us, Jesus, to forgive those who hurt us.

Teach your children

Parents are a child's first teachers. As such, it's up to them to introduce God, faith and prayer into a young one's life. Imaginative parents can think of ways to accomplish this.

One method might be the use of food. All children comprehend the delights of food. Jesus knew this as well, thus He gave Himself to us in the form of bread and wine.

One parent asked his children to tell him what pizza told them about God. Several ideas surfaced. "Pizza is round, so God is eternal." "Pizza is fun, so God likes a party." "Pizza fills us up, therefore God provides." "Pizza brings us together, so God loves our family."

You get the idea. It's literally food for thought. Varied and unlimited are the ways we can bring God into our lives.

He had been made known to them in the breaking of the bread. (Luke 24:35)

Remind me, Lord, to use the imagination You gave me.

Choices, choices

Every day, each of us faces choices. Some decisions come easily. Others take a bit more thought.

A poster in the back of a New England church spoke specifically to the young among us, listing helpful steps to making good and loving choices. Here is what that poster said:

● Find a quiet place to think about what you must do.

● Pray to the Holy Spirit for help in making a good and loving choice.

● Think about all the choices, good and bad, that you can make.

● After thinking about each one, ask: "If I do this, will it show I love God? others? myself?" If the answer is "yes" to loving God and others and myself, then it is a good choice.

● Talk over all your choices with someone who can help: a parent, teacher, aunt, uncle or older relative.

● With God's help, choose to do the right and loving thing.

> **Choose life so that you and your descendants may live, loving the Lord your God, obeying Him, and holding fast to Him; for that means life to you and length of days. (Deuteronomy 30:19-20)**

Lord, help me to always choose the right thing.

Learning to respect differences

The doctors and nurses at the King's Highway Division of Beth Israel Medical Center have noticed an increase of patients from various immigrant groups, including many who were devoutly religious. Each group has different needs.

Orthodox Jews cannot ring for a nurse on the Sabbath because that is considered work. Muslims permit only family members to touch the body of a dying person, who must be turned towards Mecca.

The staff, who are mostly Catholic or Protestant, needed to understand the various needs of their patients. Supervisors at the hospital developed fact sheets to help the staff understand the diets, organ transplant beliefs and death practices of various religions.

"By learning . . . you become more sensitive," said nurse Lydia Gonzalez. "You always have to be open to other people's needs and fill them as best you can."

Education is the key to breaking down barriers.

(The lawyer) answered, 'You shall love . . . your neighbor as yourself.' And (Jesus) said '. . . do this and you will live.' (Luke 10:27,28)

Open my eyes to see what my neighbors and I have in common, Lord of the Nations.

The simplicity of stories

As children, we loved hearing stories. It's how we learned. That's also how Christ taught, by telling stories.

One day an eight-year-old girl told her grandparents about a man named John. Seems he was a righteous man who started each day with a simple prayer: "Good morning, Lord, this is John. Please be with me this day." Eventually, on the day John was dying in his hospital bed, there came a voice that only he could hear: "Good morning, dear John, this is the Lord. Indeed I have been with you all days. And this day you shall be with Me — in Paradise."

And with that, the little girl told her grandfather, "Now I say it every day, Pop-Pop. 'Good morning, Lord, this is Becky. Please be with me this day.'"

Simple stories, simple prayers, simple love. That is perhaps what it's all about in this world.

Say to the Lord, 'My refuge and my fortress; my God, in whom I trust.' . . . He will cover you with His pinions, and under His wings you will find refuge. (Psalm 91:2,4)

Master Storyteller, be with me and bless me this day.

An ounce of prevention

In Colorado, an innovative and inspired method of preventing homelessness has been in place for the past year.

Residents can mark a box on their individual income tax return and 100% of the money collected goes to prevent homelessness. The plan is simple: provide funding to help families in danger of losing their homes *before* they become homeless.

According to Carol Breslau, Homeless Prevention Initiative Coordinator from the Colorado Trust, "In most cases, less than $300 can mean the difference between maintaining a stable home environment and becoming homeless . . . but because of a job loss or medical emergency, they are at risk of becoming homeless."

Each year the Homeless Prevention Fund helps hundreds of families stay in their homes. That's more cost effective than social services, and preserves dignity and hope.

Indeed, there's a respectful solution to every problem.

'As you did it to one of the least of these who are members of My family, you did it to Me.' (Matthew 25:40)

Be a guest in my home, Lord, and a visitor at every meal.

Doing the right thing

"Luck is the residue of design," is the famous phrase coined by the late Branch Rickey, baseball executive. It captures his pragmatism.

He made his place in history by signing Jackie Robinson to a major-league baseball contract 50 years ago, breaking the "color line" that had excluded African-Americans from the game. Rickey initially professed no great interest in social justice: "I simply wanted to win a pennant for the Brooklyn Dodgers, and I wanted the best human beings I could find to help me win it."

As he and Robinson grew closer, Rickey gave more attention to the race issue. This conservative midwestern Methodist pressed for government action on civil rights. Later, Rickey would say his initial reason for hiring Robinson was "good and sufficient. However, . . . it wasn't the whole truth."

Still, Branch Rickey not only did the right thing, he was open to learning and evolving as a human being. And the residue of his design benefitted not just a sport, but a country.

There is no longer Jew or Greek . . . slave or free . . . male and female; for all of you are one in Christ Jesus. (Galatians 3:28)

God of all, help us to be color blind.

Keeping things in perspective

Every year, as April 15 draws near, Holtsville, New York — a small village on Long Island, home for about 10,000 people — receives mail from millions.

Home to the Internal Revenue Service Center, Holtsville is the spot to which millions direct their federal income tax returns.

Postmaster Harald Aukland notes: "Without the I.R.S. Center, our certified mail would be about 20 or 30 pieces. During one week in April, we receive 20,000 to 30,000 pieces a day."

David Ceng, owner of a take-out Chinese restaurant, reports that "Fridays are the busiest days." Deli owner Steve Prisco also reports a boom in business.

But once the tax rush is over, things get pretty much back to normal for this sleepy town.

Holtsville, then, parallels our own lives. After the storms of bad times and the excitement of the good our lives, for the most part, are pretty much routine. Happily so.

There is nothing better for mortals than to eat and drink, and find enjoyment in their toil. (Ecclesiastes 2:24-25)

Lord, help me find You in the everyday.

Trading in a golf club for a hammer

During the past several years, a golf club is not the only thing championship golfer Betsy King has been swinging. She has also been found swinging a hammer, helping Habitat for Humanity construct homes in Arizona, Tennessee and North Carolina.

Recently, she even recruited fellow golfers to build a house in Charlotte, North Carolina. As storms lashed the area, the crew kept hammering. "I remember standing in a downpour, putting up siding with Betsy and laughing at the water coming off our heads," recalls Ellen Braswell, a single mom who moved into that newly-built house. "I was sorry to see her go."

King says that she has acquired a new perspective "when I see people who are not as fortunate as I have been."

Is today the day you put your life into perspective?

With gratitude in your hearts sing psalms, hymns, and spiritual songs to God. (Colossians 3:16)

Dear God, help me to know and do Your will each day.

Creative comfort

Back in 1790, Congress passed the first copyright law, and in 1800 established the Library of Congress. It was forward thinking by our founding Fathers! Who could have conceived, at a time when Paul Revere on horseback was the quickest way to send a message, that Americans would ever be traveling on an "information superhighway"?

Thanks to that groundwork and an 1870 law, creative works can be registered and protected by the Library of Congress. In 1994 alone, there were 530,000 claims to copyright, 757,000 works were received and $204 million in royalties were distributed to copyright holders.

What you believe, feel, speculate about on paper, or even on your computer screen, is important. Innovation, rational thinking, thorough research all play a part in developing your ideas. Let your creative light shine!

In the beginning was the Word. (John 1:1)

Open my eyes to see, my heart to feel, and my mouth to speak Thy praises, Word made flesh.

Cows on the air!

Dairy and beef cattle on giant agri-business farms must receive antibiotics to prevent diseases. And a federal law requires a waiting period before they can then be sold for human food.

The Food and Drug Administration became aware that some people were breaking this law. But how to catch them?

They decided to implant transponders in the cattle and sell them to the suspects.

A first try with Buttercup failed.

Redesigned transponders — radios — that opened like umbrellas inside Buttercup, and Elsie and Elmer proved successful. A sting operation was established. It was said the cattle had been treated with antibiotics (they hadn't really).

FDA agents followed the transponders inside Buttercup, Elsie and Elmer. They *were* sold for human food. The owners of Buttercup, Elsie and Elmer went to trial for selling adulterated food.

Remember, there is always a way to solve a problem. It just takes ingenuity.

An excellent spirit, knowledge, and understanding to interpret dreams, explain riddles, and solve problems were found in this Daniel. (Daniel 5:12)

Thank You, Lord, for the gift of human ingenuity and intelligence.

A messenger of hope

When Victoria Cummock of Coral Gables, Florida, heard about the bombing of the Federal Building in Oklahoma City, her first reaction was: Go there.

Having survived her own tragedy — her husband, John, died aboard Pan Am Flight 103 when the plane exploded over Lockerbie, Scotland — Victoria is convinced of the need to help others get through similar circumstances.

"Really, what I do is to talk with people," she said. "I listen to the widows and widowers, to the parents who are having nightmares about raising children by themselves. And I can say to them, 'Yeah, that happened to me.'"

Victoria knows firsthand how such caring conversations can help. Shortly after Lockerbie, a woman in London called to see how she was doing. That woman had lost her own husband in the bombing of a London department store. She told Victoria that it would get better. It did.

"It is so important to see that other people who have been where you are have managed to live a full life again," Victoria said.

Support the weak. (Acts 20:35)

Lord, help me to be a messenger of strength and hope for others.

Our green home

Every April 20 is Earth Day. A day to encourage responsible stewardship, even love, for this little planet which is our home.

But what can you do on the 364 days between one Earth Day and the next?

Park that car. Walk, bike, bus, train to your destination.

Ask, "Do I really need to buy this?" Bring your own reusable shopping bag. Keep to a shopping list. Encourage yourself to spend less than last month, than last year.

Reuse. Repair. Refurbish. Update.

Get out into parks. On lakes and rivers. Alone, or with friends and family.

Be involved in community decisions that affect your environment. And other's.

Teach. Children and teens. Your peers.

It's never too early or too late to live Earth Day every day. Nor is it ever too early or too late to interest others in living Earth Day every day.

The Lord . . . formed the earth and made it (He established it; He did not create it a chaos, He formed it to be inhabited!). (Isaiah 45:18)

Blessed are You, Creator, for all earth's beauty and wonders!

Coffee and conduct

Starbucks Coffee is a business success story. It is also a company with a conscience, one concerned not just with the quality of its products but with the quality of its conduct as well.

David Olsen, a Starbucks senior vice-president, instituted a company code of conduct, a statement of beliefs for doing business. The impetus behind it? "To live up to our sense of responsibility to make a difference in the world," says Olsen. According to the statement, Starbucks:

■ Respects human rights and dignity . . .

■ Works with others to raise standards of health, education, safety and economic well-being . . .

■ Believes in diversity and respects different cultures . . .

■ Helps preserve and enhance the physical environment.

We all have a responsibility to leave this world a better place. Value not just profits, but people and the environment we all share.

In the path of righteousness there is life, in walking its path there is no death. (Proverbs 12:38)

Jesus, help me to conduct myself responsibly and conscientiously.

Well-placed trust

Lloyd's of London, the famous insurance association, has insured nearly everything.

It insured Jimmy Durante's nose and Fred Astaire's legs. It insured the first airplane and America's first astronaut. It has insured people against a golf opponent's making a hole in one, and against death caused by a falling satellite.

One of its most intriguing policies was a "happiness policy" that insured against "worry lines" developing on a model's face.

There's a better kind of happiness insurance: trusting God. It can prevent needless worries and fears.

Happy are those who trust in the Lord. (Proverbs 16:20)

Enable me to trust You, Savior. Remind me to be wise as a serpent and innocent as a dove with others and self.

Hero of Heartbreak Hotel

Heroes are made, not born. James Ray is, by anybody's definition, a hero. Shot down over North Vietnam, Ray spent two years in Hanoi's notorious Heartbreak Hotel.

During that time of physical and mental torture, Ray and his fellow prisoners memorized whole sections of the Bible because the Communists would not allow them to read the Scriptures more than one hour a week.

"They seemed afraid of the Scriptures, as if they sensed the spiritual help kept us from breaking."

The physical deprivations increased their spirituality. They pooled their talents and helped each other, developing a true community of caring and support. By the time they regained their freedom, James Ray was convinced that "compassion and responsibility go hand in hand."

One does not live by bread alone, but by every word that comes from the mouth of the Lord. (Deuteronomy 8:3)

Lord, help me see Your gift in every event.

Personal initiative

Annie Plummer, of Savannah, is the city's "Dictionary Lady."

Ms. Plummer, a grandmother who cleans buildings for a living, noticed that schoolchildren crossing at a busy intersection near her home had no books.

Concerned, she bought 30 pocket dictionaries with her own money and gave them out to students.

A local newscaster publicized her effort and donations began coming in to help her buy dictionaries.

Now, four years later, she has given away more than 17,000 copies to students.

The mayor of Savannah, a personal supporter of the project, said of Ms. Plummer: "Here's a lady who didn't wait for government to do the job."

She encouraged each of them.
(2 Maccabees 7:21)

Show adults how to encourage young people,
Jesus of Nazareth.

Sound silence

In her book, *Gift From the Sea,* Anne Morrow Lindbergh writes: "If one sets aside time for a business appointment or a social engagement, that time is accepted as inviolable."

"But," she continues, "if anyone says, 'I cannot come because that is my hour to be alone,' one is considered rude, egotistical or strange . . ."

In the hectic, fast-paced world in which most of us live and work, learning to be still and silent is often not that easy.

Yet "switching off," says Dr. Stephan Rechtschaffen, author of *Time Shifting: A Guide to Creating More Time for Your Life,* is essential. "Once you learn to shift your own internal rhythm at will," he says, "It gets easier to function in a hectic world."

It is very often in moments of silent contemplation that we can sort out situations and relationships in our lives. Get a new perspective on a problem you face, and really get in touch with who you are — and Who is always with you.

Be still before the Lord, and wait patiently for Him. (Psalm 37:7)

Lord, You probe the silence of our hearts; give me the strength to be still.

Mercy is their middle name

Mist was still clinging to the tips of the trees as the first morning light was reflected from the wings of the mercy plane.

Pacing in customs, Sister Bertilla McNeeley eagerly awaited the fifteen volunteer health professionals and the cartons of medical supplies they had brought with them for the hospital in San Juan de Dios in Nicaragua.

This volunteer hospital was founded in 1992 to serve the poorest people in Granada, Nicaragua — population 165,000 — by an office of the New Orleans Archdiocese.

The hospital was damaged in the recent Civil War. There is little equipment. Electricity is intermittent. There are holes in the roof.

With it all, an overworked staff battles malnutrition, dengue fever, malaria and cholera. And the hospital is a glowing candle of hope.

This world is filled with people — near and far — who need your help. Do all you can.

You received without payment; give without payment. (Matthew 10:8)

Lord, help me to do all that I can do and to see the need to do it.

Raise your hand and volunteer

When we were in grade school, before we began to worry about what people would think of us, the teacher would ask who would erase the board. Hands would shoot into the air to say, "I'll do it!"

As we grew up, we didn't want to be considered a goody-two-shoes, so we stopped volunteering. Yet it is, I think, basic to human nature to help out. In today's hectic and fast paced society, it is sometimes difficult to volunteer. Our personal time is just so precious. There is little time for helping at school, church or community. Still, there are times when the importance of the need outweighs the inconvenience.

Studies have proven that volunteers reap the rewards of better health, increased energy and, most of all, a sense of euphoria. Helping out, pitching in, volunteering, is a wonderful tonic for both the body and the soul.

Instead of worrying how we can find the time to do it, maybe we should just do it.

We can say with confidence, 'The Lord is my helper, I will not be afraid. What can anyone do to me?' (Hebrews 13:6)

Increase my capacity to see need and respond, Merciful Savior.

Knit one, purl two, knit . . .

Bill Hochhaus is a great bear of a man. He looks more the picture of the hardy fisherman or sailor than anyone else. Until 1976 he smoked.

Then a friend, Jessica, wanted to help him stop smoking. So she gave him one knitting lesson. Now Hochhaus knits instead of smoking.

Hochhaus measures long trips by the number of hats knitted. He has taken knitting lessons and whipped-up intricately knitted items for friends and relatives.

And, fearing he was the only man in knitting's sorority, he was relieved to learn that a man named Kaffe is "one of the best knitters in the world." He began a knitting circle in his home to teach knitting to women. And admits that it's a good way to meet possible dates.

If you are open to the unusual, you can often find enjoyment while solving problems major and minor.

A friend loves at all times. (Proverbs 17:17)

Bless me with friends who will help me overcome my unhealthy habits, Jesus.

An aerial clown

Are you constantly amazed at the variety of God's creation?

The pelican certainly is one of nature's funniest looking flying creatures. Its large, oversized beak can hold three gallons of water and many fish. Yet this seemingly clumsy looking creature can dive into the water from a height of 33 feet, fill its pouch and maneuver to the surface with all the grace of a ballet dancer.

Pelicans are great parents, and spend most of their time feeding their clutch of chicks, usually three in number. An adult pelican needs about 4 lbs. of fish a day, but chicks need about 150 lbs. during their three month nesting period. Both parents share the task of caring for the chicks.

Thanks to bans on DDT and careful monitoring, all six species of pelicans are off the endangered list. Pelicans show God's wisdom and sense of humor.

What else do you see in nature?

God gave Solomon very great wisdom, discernment, and breath of understanding . . . He would speak of . . . birds, and reptiles, and fish. (1 Kings 4:29,33)

Give us the insight, Holy Spirit, to find the humor and the wisdom in Your Creation.

A pride of literary lions

The Post Office has begun issuing stamps honoring American writers as part of their Literary Arts stamp series. One of the newest inductees into this pantheon of philatelism is novelist and short-story writer, F. Scott Fitzgerald.

Fitzgerald and his wife, Zelda, are considered by many to be the epitome of the Jazz Age. Several of his stories, including his most accomplished novel, "The Great Gatsby," give a vivid depiction of the America of that era.

F. Scott Fitzgerald joined noted authors of the last two centuries: James Thurber, Dorothy Parker, William Saroyan, Marianne Moore, Ernest Hemingway, William Faulkner, T. S. Eliot, Herman Melville, Nathaniel Hawthorne, Edith Wharton and John Steinbeck.

Your portrait may never grace a commemorative postage stamp. But who could argue that the most important thing to be remembered for is good deeds and an ethical life.

(The Most High) repays mortals according to their deeds. (Sirach 35:24)

Enable me to live a truly memorable life, Holy Spirit.

Reach out to others

E. M. Forster captured an essential yearning of the human condition when he wrote, "Only connect." We all need to connect with something that transcends our fragile selves, to find a vision and a set of values that gives meaning to daily life.

Best-selling author Sam Keen suggests that one way to achieve this is by incorporating joyous rituals into our lives. By creating a spiritual practice built around a calendar that recognizes our own personal holy days and celebrations throughout the year, we stand a good chance of recovering the sense of the sacred that is missing. For example, Keen has named his own set of days, such as "Family Day," "Lilac Day," and "Friend's Day." He's become a "connoisseur of gratitude," pausing frequently in his day to give thanks.

The spiritual journey is one we take alone, yet together. Reach out with your soul and connect with your community.

Rejoice before the Lord . . . you and your sons and your daughters, your male and female slaves, the Levites . . . as well as the strangers, the orphans, and the widows . . . among you. (Deuteronomy 16:11)

Jesus, help me to enjoy the spirit of community.

Simply charming

It must have been a simpler age which spawned the charming tradition of button gathering.

Memory strips. Button strings. Charm strings. There are several names and legends associated with the 19th century custom which encouraged young women to collect and string buttons. Getting 999 buttons was significant since the 1,000th would be added by "Prince Charming."

"Button" seems an inadequate description for the small objects made in a variety of materials and designs: ivory, brass, pewter, china. One collector discovered a charm string with "a tintype of a young girl, a micromosaic of Roman ruins . . . a Confederate infantry eagle."

Individual buttons are interesting, yet some collectors find the entire string fascinating for the biographical tales it tells.

As with photo albums, families could share stories about where and when the buttons had been acquired. One 90-year-old woman's collection offered reminders of her studies, her marriage and her honeymoon abroad.

Don't neglect the past in trying to understand the present.

The memory of the righteous is a blessing. (Proverbs 10:7)

God, help us appreciate life's simple pleasures.

Honoring our elders

We stand to learn much from Native Americans, especially with regard to the elderly.

At the San Xavier del Bac mission near Tucson, Arizona, Betty Calvert observed how her 94-year-old mother, frail and small, moved among other worshipers, most of whom were Indians.

Betty watched as her mother approached and the Indians dropped to their knees to ask for her blessing. Some whispered, "Vaya con dios" (Go with God) as she made the sign of the cross over them, while her daughter looked on in amazement.

Later, at home, Calvert's mother told her, "The Indians . . . revere their elders. They believe all the wisdom and knowledge an old person has acquired can be passed on through a blessing or a loving touch."

What a lovely belief. It's not too late to learn from our elders and ask for their blessing.

Rise before the aged, and defer to the old. (Leviticus 19:32)

Jesus, help us to learn from those who have come before us.

We are all hunters

Jim Loehr, sports psychologist, has analyzed the performance of Greg Norman at the 1996 Masters tournament with some interesting observations. Norman, one of the world's best golfers, was in the lead by 6 strokes. The only thing which could defeat him was himself. And defeated he was.

Loehr sees being the hunted rather than the hunter a disaster waiting to happen. He feels that being in the lead makes it psychologically harder to concentrate, to make your genius shine. If you are leading, everyone is after you. You can lose your aggressive edge by playing it safe.

It's the same in the workplace, the home, school. Perhaps it would be better if we played "ourselves" and not someone else. Perhaps it is possible to win even though you lose. Everywhere in life there are dilemmas. Some we handle, some we don't. Trying makes the difference.

Their only plan is to bring down a person of prominence. They take pleasure in falsehood; they bless with their mouths, but inwardly they curse. For God alone my soul waits . . . my hope is from Him. (Psalm 62:4-5)

Give my eye clarity of vision and my arm strength of purpose, Holy Spirit.

Lessons in love

The Rev. Daniel F. Miner outlines six lessons in love which he says are hard to carry out but rewarding once actually applied.

Rev. Miner suggests we resolve:

1. Not to use the expression "if only." As in, "If only my life were better . . ." Instead of feeling sorry for ourselves we need to try to be grateful.

2. To stop complaining about our misfortunes and life situations.

3. Not to blame other people for our unhappiness. Attempts to control, manipulate and blame others end in frustration. It's ourselves we must learn to change.

4. Not to blame other people for our loneliness. We must do the reaching out and avoid self-pity.

5. That if we are ever to find happiness in our relationships, avoid loneliness and self-pity, we must change ourselves.

6. That the way to live is a life of Christian love.

It is possible to be a more loving person. If only we make the effort.

God is love, and those who abide in love abide in God, and God abides in them. (1 John 4:16)

Jesus, please instruct us in Your loving ways.

Passing along the secret of success

George Paris has found a down-to-earth way to help the elderly in his community.

Paris, himself 80 years old, grows vegetables on his Tuskegee, Alabama, farm and gives them to needy senior citizens.

This retired farm loan officer is an expert in both agriculture and economics. He understands how difficult it is for seniors to live on Social Security checks. So he gives them the vegetables he grows. He also teaches them how to grow their own.

Long active in the civil rights movement and now an advocate for senior rights, he still finds time for gardening.

He says, "I feel the Lord still has more for me to do. So I'm going to keep on 'til He calls me home."

The Lord will be your confidence. (Proverbs 3:26)

Be my confidence, Lord, my stronghold against pessimism and despair.

G-Men

A special force of trash collectors across the country have been dubbed "G-Men" for their volunteer crime fighting as well as trash collecting actions.

They've been trained to scan city streets for suspicious activity and report it to their dispatchers, who call the police. The program began in Aurora, Colorado, and has spread to cities in Utah, Texas, and Massachusetts.

It makes sense that people who work outside all day would notice strange happenings in the neighborhood; as G-Man Patrick Shockley says, "We see everything that goes on out there."

A thoughtful and creative person came up with this idea to fight crime. What ideas can you come up with to help your community? Don't keep your thoughts to yourself. Talk to your neighbors and take action.

At the same time, be cautious. Don't make hasty judgments.

Give the members of your community a fair hearing, and judge rightly between one person and another, whether citizen or resident alien. You must not be partial in judging. (Deuteronomy 1:16-17)

Deliver us from rash judgments, Just Judge.

In sickness and in health

A month after Victoria Ingram-Curlee married Randee Curlee, a severe diabetic, she donated one of her kidneys to her new husband.

Unfortunately, her husband took a turn for the worse, eventually losing his eyesight. Moreover, the strong drugs he takes have adversely affected his moods. "So he takes it out on me a lot," says Mrs. Ingram-Curlee. "I have to stand in there and say, 'I will not tolerate this.'"

Despite her sacrifice and the difficulties she's endured, the donor insists she'd do it all again. She loves her husband, and the transplant has extended his life and given him new energy.

The path of love and marriage is never storybook smooth. For some, the potholes of life are deep. Consequently, declares Victoria Ingram-Curlee, "I constantly pray for the ability to understand."

Whatever our problems, talking to God never hurts. Some days, it may be the only thing that really helps.

Ask, and it will be given you; search, and you will find; knock, and the door will be opened for you. (Matthew 7:7)

Help us, Lord God, to persevere on life's rough road.

The gift of children

Pulitzer Prize-winning writer Anna Quindlan shocked the journalism community when she announced her decision to quit her job to stay home with her children. Quindlan was a highly-respected columnist with the New York Times who once said she would never have children because she wanted to rise to the top unencumbered.

Colleagues and readers were surprised at Quindlan's about-face decision. But having children made her realize the important things in life.

Quindlan says of her children: "They have given me perspective on the pursuit of joy and the passage of time. I miss too much when I am out of their orbit, and as they grow, like a time-lapse photograph that makes a flower out of a bud in scant minutes, I understand that I will have time to pursue a more frantic agenda when they have gone on to pursue their own. But they have made a more frantic agenda seem somehow less seductive than a satisfying one."

Children are God's gifts.

Praise your God, O Zion! . . . He blesses your children within you. (Psalm 147:12,13)

Thank You, Author of Life, for the gift of children.

On duty and decency

Jimmy Breslin is a journalist with a talent for capturing the heart of a story and the people who live it. When his wife Rosemary died a number of years ago, he gave a eulogy that showed the kind of decent person she was. He said:

"She was a person who regarded life as one long attempt to provide a happy moment or so for another person . . .

"She thought the word duty meant that each day there should be a word or a gesture that would cause someone else to smile over the life about them. Her contempt was reserved for those who would not attempt this. Who are you, she would rail, to go through a day knowing that another day is to follow and another day after that . . . and still you refuse to join with us and help soften the path of those around you?"

It is so easy to think only of what we want. But we jostle through life in the company of others. That is the path God set before us all.

The Lord is my shepherd . . . He leads me in right paths for His name's sake.
(Psalm 23:1,3)

Why do I need to be reminded so often of my brother's need, my sister's hope? Lord, help us help each other.

The power of forgiveness

When Elizabeth Barrett married fellow poet Robert Browning, her parents disapproved so strongly that they disowned her.

Elizabeth wrote frequently to her parents, expressing her love and wish for a reconciliation. Even though she got no reply, she continued writing. Finally, about ten years after her marriage, she received a box from her parents. In it, she found all the letters she had written to them — still unopened.

Later generations reading these letters have been moved by their expressiveness. If her parents had read them, their hearts might have been softened and the family reunited.

Harboring resentment can only cause pain. But forgiveness heals.

Forgive us our debts as we have forgiven our debtors. (Matthew 6:12)

Dear God, forgiveness is often next to impossible. But, help me to forgive for love of You — and for my own good.

What is youth?

Most people would say that youth is a time of life when we're young. That's not what General Douglas MacArthur would have said.

On his 75th birthday, General MacArthur explained his view of youth as being more of a state of mind. "It is not wholly a matter of ripe cheeks. It is a temper of the will, a quality of the imagination, a vigor of the emotions, a freshness of the deep springs of life."

The general said youth "means a temperamental predominance of courage over timidity, of an appetite for adventure over love of ease. Nobody grows old by merely living a number of years."

Years don't age one beyond the surface. What really takes a toll and "wrinkles the soul," said MacArthur, are "worry, doubt, self-distrust, fear and despair."

Pessimism and cynicism age us. What keeps our hearts young are "messages of beauty, hope, cheer and courage."

In a culture that seems to glorify youth and stigmatize age, it is heartening to consider the things of the mind and soul that really matter.

Keep up your courage. (Acts 27:25)

Help me, Jesus, to more fully appreciate the rewards of maintaining a youthful spirit.

You never know who is watching

At 18, Ivan Seidenberg was a janitor.

Today, he is Chairman and Chief Executive Officer of the NYNEX Telephone Company.

Whom does Seidenberg credit with his start on the road to success? Mike, the superintendent of the New York City office building where he had been janitor. "Mike said little but watched everything very carefully," he recalled.

One day Mike asked Seidenberg about a book he was reading, and he told the older man that he was putting himself through college at night. In reponse, Mike simply said, "Okay," and walked away. But months later, Mike gave Seidenberg information on companies that would help pay for tuition — including the telephone company.

"Except for 22 months in the Army, I have worked at the telephone company . . . ever since," Seidenberg said, adding: "Mike gave me a helping hand. If you take pride in your work and do a good job, you never know who might be watching and one day provide a boost."

**There is nothing better for mortals than to . . . find enjoyment in their toil.
(Ecclesiastes 2:24)**

Lord, may I always use all the talents You gave me.

Know that name?

English word origins come from a great variety of sources. Many languages add to its richness. But some words actually derive from the names of individuals.

Among these eponyms, one of the best known is *sandwich*. It is named for the fourth Earl of Sandwich who supposedly invented this hand-held meal so he would not have to leave the gambling table.

If you think something is a *doozy* it is because of Frederick Duesenberg. The auto maker's 1932 roadster had a powerful 320-horsepower engine and could go an impressive 130 miles per hour.

Next time you read a book *blurb* think of Belinda Blurb. She modeled for the cover of a 1906 book of humor by Gelett Burgess. Somehow her name stuck to the words on the jacket.

Try to make your name synonymous with integrity and kindness. Then the good you do will last even longer than any name or fame.

A good name is to be chosen rather than great riches. (Proverbs 22:1)

May people who hear my name praise Yours, Lord, for the blessings You help me share with them in all I am and do.

Standing tall for kids

Basketball player Joe Dumars learned about community responsibility early in life. When he was a child in Natchitoches, Louisiana, Dumars' father made a basketball hoop out of an old door and a bicycle rim. Every kid in the neighborhood came out to play — and his mother made sure that everyone felt welcome.

Now a guard for the Detroit Pistons, Dumars is still bringing hope to young people. Every year he hosts a celebrity tennis tournament which benefits Detroit's Children's Hospital, and sponsors a basketball camp for disadvantaged and disabled kids.

Dumars is a young athlete who has become a role model. He says he learned it from his family. "Growing up," he says, "the only thing we knew was giving and sharing with others."

Today's kids need to learn about giving and sharing with those less fortunate if they are going to make tomorrow's world a better place. Aim to be a positive role model to the young people in your life.

**The righteous walk in integrity — happy are the children who follow them!
(Proverbs 20:7)**

Let us be good examples to children, Father.

How to get ahead

How many articles have we read about being successful, in school or on the job?

George Washington Carver could have written his own book on getting ahead. Born of slave parents in Missouri, he left the farm where he was born at the age of 10. Eventually he settled in Kansas and worked his way through high school.

Following his college graduation in 1894 at the age of 30, he joined the faculty at Iowa State College of Agriculture and continued his studies. Before his death in 1943, Carver had established himself as an outstanding educator and an award-winning innovator in the field of agricultural sciences.

But for Carver, the secret of success was not found in books or articles or college courses. Carver said: "How far you go in life depends on your being tender with the young, compassionate with the aged, sympathetic with the striving, and tolerant of the weak and the strong — because someday you will have been all of these."

I have become all things to all people, that I might . . . save some. (1 Corinthians 9:22)

Dear God, help me to realize Your greatest lessons are woven into the fabric of life's experiences.

It's a long way to push a dream

George Jackson was 17 when he left Florida in 1941 with nothing but a dream. One morning he got up and decided to move to New York. Within three days he was down to 65 cents and no job. But he was young and fearless. Finally, he got a job as a delivery boy for a laundry on Amsterdam Avenue.

He had a lot of jobs over the next 55 years. Today George Jackson has lost some of his youth, but none of his fearless optimism. Today, he is owner of Manhattan's only portable night club. It's a cart he pushes up and down Broadway. In the well of the cart is a CD-player that broadcasts selections from "That Old Feeling," Jackson's CD, which he sells for $15. He is making music. "This is something I always wanted to do, though — not pushing a cart but getting my music out there." He still has his dreams. Dreams are healthy for all of us.

I will pour out My spirit on all flesh; your sons and your daughters shall prophesy, your old men shall dream dreams, and your young men shall see visions. (Joel 2:28)

Give me courage, O Lord, to pursue Your ways unceasingly.

Living with technology

Are we losing jobs and wages to technology? Moving toward an homogenization of commerce and culture? Living at an inhuman pace? Warehousing children in day care? Our elders, too?

Or, is technology making life more humane?

At the dawn of the Industrial Revolution in England, the Luddites violently protested the use of machines and the establishment of factories. They lost their war.

Recently their philosophical descendants raised these same questions. But in keeping with a Plain Quaker tradition they talked about a "revolution of hearts." They avoid violence, offensive activism, judgmentalism and criticism.

They want to ease the "bad habits" of technology "out of the house" gradually. They suggest making technology a "condiment," not the entree at the banquet of life.

We humans must use our God-given intelligence to make technology the servant, not the master.

The protection of wisdom is like the protection of money and the advantage of knowledge is that wisdom gives life to the one who possesses it. (Ecclesiastes 7:12)

Holy Spirit, make us wise.

Genuine winners

Tennis pro Linda Wild used to become very upset when she lost a match. She would throw her racket against the fence or leave the court crying. She felt that losing a match meant she was a failure.

Wild doesn't feel that way anymore. Religious faith has changed her perspective. She understands that winning and losing are both part of life. They don't affect her worth as a person. She knows that she is always important to God.

We are all more than the game we play, more than whatever we do. We are all special, with unique God-given qualities.

Whatever life brings, we can be winners in the true sense when we recognize our value as children of God.

I have called you by name, you are Mine . . . you are precious in My sight, and honored, and I love you. (Isaiah 43:1,4)

People and life's circumstances sometimes make me doubt or forget my true worth. At those times, Lord and Lover, remind me that I am Your beloved.

Careful: the children are watching

The best way to teach our children to care about others is by our example. In your church, find programs for which you can volunteer with your children. Make it active and personal. If your church doesn't have any such programs, look around in your community. Some examples:

■ Participate in "walks" to raise money for causes.

■ Volunteer to bring food to local soup kitchens or to shut-ins.

■ Begin food drives for the needy or disaster relief.

■ Visit nursing homes. Seniors love having children visit.

■ Participate in neighborhood clean-ups.

■ Encourage your children to find age-appropriate avenues of service as they grow.

The sooner we can instill into our children how connected we are to each other, the sooner the world will be a better place.

The children of this age are more shrewd in dealing with their own generation than the children of light. (Luke 16:8)

Keep my eyes bright, my back strong and my enthusiasm that of a child, Jesus.

Some burn, many build

In the spring of 1994 three white teenagers set fire to a black church in Mississippi, destroying it. People in the area — blacks and whites — immediately launched an effort to rebuild the church.

Donations of money and supplies poured in, as well as volunteer labor. Media coverage of the story brought additional support from all over the country. More than 300 volunteers helped with the rebuilding.

The great outpouring of support did much to heal the wound caused by the destruction of the church. As one local minister observed, "The warmth of God's love is always more powerful than the heat of human hatred."

When we care about others and help them, we become instruments of God's healing love.

Hatred stirs up strife, but love covers all offenses. (Proverbs 10:12)

Father, heal our hatreds; mend the wounds our hatred has caused.

Real joy is an inside job

Spanish moss, the gray plant we see draped from the branches of trees in the South, is a misunderstood plant.

It's often thought to be a parasitic moss that takes its food from the trees it grows on. Actually, it isn't a moss at all. It's an epiphyte — a nonparasitic plant that makes its own nourishment from the air.

The false assumptions about this plant bring to mind our misconceptions about happiness. We think of it as depending on our circumstances — on fame or fortune, health or beauty.

But we make our own happiness. Real joy comes from within. When we trust God, knowing that He is with us, we have an inner peace that sustains us, no matter how much turmoil life may bring.

Joy has come to me from the Holy One. (Baruch 4:22)

Savior, give us the wisdom and courage to find our joy in You alone.

A photographer, children — hope

Beginning in 1994 Rwanda, in east central Africa, was engulfed by a horrific war between two tribal groups, the Hutus and Tutsis. Thousands were slaughtered.

Thousands more fled for their lives. Often at night. Always in panic. Family members became separated.

Of the approximately 100,000 lost children, 12,000 found their way to UNICEF-sponsored camps. It didn't seem as though these children and their families could be reunited.

Then a photographer whose professional name is Reza became part of the solution. He collected donated film and cameras. He trained volunteer photographers. And he set up open air photo galleries. By October 1996, 3,500 children had been found by their families.

Reza says, "If you don't care what happens, what kind of person are you?"

One photographer used his skills to help solve a problem. Do we use ours?

Religion that is pure and undefiled before God, the Father, is this: to care for orphans and widows in their distress. (James 1:27)

Master, thank You for my many skills. Help me use them for Your honor and the good of my sisters and brothers.

Kids making a difference

A Maryland teenager is using her spare time to help those in need — and is getting other young people to help, too.

Amber Coffman, 14, is the founder of Happy Helpers for the Homeless, a group of volunteers aged 6 to 19 who give food and compassion to Baltimore's homeless. They meet every weekend in Amber's apartment to make 400 lunches and then they distribute them in front of City Hall. The enthusiastic teenager has gotten local businesses to contribute bread and pastries.

Amber learned about helping others at an early age — at 8, she volunteered with her mom at a homeless shelter. Three years later, she wrote a report on Mother Teresa and it spurred her to want to spend her life serving the needy. "She really inspired me," says Amber. "I realized there was a big need right here."

Encourage a child you know to help others.

**And a little child shall lead them.
(Isaiah 11:6)**

Father, guide us to be living examples of goodness, so that our children may follow.

The man who brought the war home

Egbert Roscoe Murrow was born April 25, 1908, in Polecate Creek, North Carolina, a hamlet with no automobiles, telephones, or electricity. In 1934 he became involved in helping to expatriate Jewish academics from an increasingly anti-Semitic Germany. In 1937 he was dispatched by CBS to London as European representative.

In 1940, Edward R. Murrow took his microphone to the London streets, making the horror of the bombings very real in American homes. His was the most trusted news voice on radio. He later attempted to facilitate himself to television, a medium he never warmed to. "This instrument can teach," he declared. "It can illuminate. Yes, and it can even inspire. But it can do so only to the extent that humans are determined to use it to those ends. Otherwise, it is merely wires and lights in a box."

He brought us the war, and a prophecy.

Prophets are not without honor except in their own country and in their own house. (Matthew 13:57)

Help me to recognize Your voice in all the voices I hear, God.

A rewarding conversation

About a decade ago, an elderly man named Ernest Randall walked into the library in the small northern Maine town of Washburn. He had a pleasant chat with librarian Barbara Porter.

Randall, it turned out, was a native of the town, although he had moved away as a young man, eventually settling in Westfield, Massachusetts.

During their conversation, Porter recalled reading about Randall in a book called *OX5 Aviation Pioneers,* and she told Randall. Indeed, Randall had been a member of those flyers until a hand injury forced him to give up flying. Randall seemed pleased that Porter knew him.

Just how pleased did not come to light until 10 years later. Town officials learned of Randall's death and his bequest to the Washburn Memorial Library of more than $91,000.

Sometimes a little kindness — and a good memory — can go a very long way.

Give graciously to all the living; do not withhold kindness even from the dead.
(Sirach 7:33)

Lord, help me be always kind to strangers and to take time to talk to someone because You're in each person.

When you're blue — try this

These are tips for you when you're feeling a little down.

■ Go for a walk in a park . . . slowly. Let the grass and the trees cheer you up.

■ Sit quietly in a church or a temple. Don't think. Just sit and let your eyes wander.

■ Tell funny stories to yourself. Laugh if you feel like it.

■ Lie on the floor, close your eyes and imagine you are flying.

■ Take a drive or walk to someplace with water, a reservoir, a lake, a river. Watch the light on the water.

The best thing to do, of course, is try to cheer up somebody else.

In any event, you'll find your life a little richer and your soul a little more buoyant by focusing on the ordinary little things of beauty.

David danced before the Lord with all his might. (2 Samuel 6:14)

Give me a song to sing and a heart to sing it, Beloved Teacher.

A real close-knit group

The idea belonged to schoolchildren in the area. That's when Pittsburgh resident, Evelyn Wright, read about it. She shared the idea with her sister, Dolores Lauer, who also got in on the act.

Before anyone realized it, 35 women were meeting regularly at St. Gerard's Church to crochet afghans for the needy. Even Evelyn's husband, John, joined the group, driving his wife — and 35 afghans with gift boxes — to a local residence for homeless and low-income women over 50.

Next to benefit from this group effort: a shelter for mothers and children.

"There's a lot of real care that goes into the process," Dolores notes.

This "knitting circle" in Pennsylvania is but one example of the good that can be accomplished when we work together.

May the God of steadfastness and encouragement grant you to live in harmony with one another . . . so that together you may . . . glorify the God and Father of our Lord Jesus Christ. (Romans 15:5,6)

Gentle and loving Father, give us the grace to trust that You are always with us, in all we do.

Viola: the sound of silence

Kim Kashkashian plays the viola, an instrument of unstandardized length whose design embodies a notoriously awkward acoustical compromise. Ms. Kashkashian coaxes from this union of wood and string hauntingly bittersweet musical tones. And when she plays — music from late baroque to modern — her eyes shine with fervor.

Of late she has been drawn to the music of Giya Kancheli, an intensely spiritual composer who values simplicity and silence. She says, "out of music comes silence, and sometimes silence itself turns into music."

There's also an intellectual and spiritual affinity between Kancheli and Ms. Kashkashian. He's from the Georgia Republic; she is of Armenian parentage. "There's an unspoke awareness of values (in his music), a certain kind of judgment-making — something you don't have to talk about out loud in order to feel really close."

Wouldn't it be wonderful if our works could be said to reflect our values? . . . our spirituality? . . . even our ancestry?

Praise Him with lute and harp! . . . Praise Him with strings and pipe! (Psalm 150:3,4)

Play Your songs on the strings of my heart, Glorious Lord.

Being a professional

Even after shattering Lou Gehrig's thought-to-be-unbreakable record of 2,130 consecutive games played, Cal Ripkin Jr., baseball's paragon of professionalism, brings dedication and devotion to the field each and every game.

At the Sullivan Street Theater in New York City's Greenwich Village a musical called "The Fantasticks" goes on and on, for over 35 years now. Bryan Hull, a 57-year-old actor, has played his part 8 times a week, 50 weeks a year, for 15 years, for a total of 6,058 performances.

What makes these professionals special is that they give their best every day. And not only because they're being paid to perform under pressure.

As Bryan Hull points out, he tries to bring something new and fresh to the part every night, because every night people are seeing him and the show for the first time.

The best we can do is to give our best each time as though it were the first time.

**Prosper the work of our hands!
(Psalm 90:17)**

Oh Lord, help me to bring my heart, mind and spirit to my daily labors.

All you need is love

It is very easy to say there isn't enough time to pray. Well, there is enough time. Maybe we only have to change our concept of prayer. Jeanne Monsees of Central Islip, a wife and mother of five, tries to focus on God when engaged in "mindless" daily chores. "God and I have some great conversations over the laundry and doing dishes."

Others manage to become involved in centering prayer, a method of contemplative prayer that involves sitting quietly for 20 minutes and focusing on God.

The most difficult part of prayer for many is just "listening." Yet conversation, to be effective, takes two. Listening for God's voice is more than politeness. Prayer time, whether it is centering prayer, quiet meditation, the rosary, or a mental conversation with God is rewarding and helpful in dealing with the demands of daily life.

God is always there . . . waiting.

Those who were ready went with him into the wedding banquet. (Matthew 25:10)

Help me to hear Your voice, O Lord, whether it be soft or loud.

Valuing the weather

Boots? Umbrella? Gloves? For many people, weather is just a useful guide for how to dress each morning. Otherwise they take it for granted.

Not farmers. Not Neighbor Tryon.

Writing about the 84-year-old farmer who had touched his life, Stephen Hyde noted in *Yankee* magazine how Neighbor Tryon had come from a family of farmers. "He recognized changing weather patterns by feel and taste and look, by how birds gossiped and how the cows behaved."

Weather was one of the most important things in Neighbor Tryon's day. Some nights the Maine native could be found re-reading old almanacs or his grandfather's diaries. Sometimes he told stories while Hyde and others "sat, absorbed, like witnesses to the Creation."

According to Hyde, his friend "died the day that the daisies blossomed."

"When it is evening, you say, 'It will be fair weather, for the sky is red.' And in the morning, 'It will be stormy today, for the sky is red and threatening.' You know how to interpret the appearance of the sky, but you cannot interpret the signs of the time."
(Matthew 16:2-3)

Help us, Lord, to appreciate the "signs of the times."

Turning a curse into a blessing

Jim Eisenreich was convinced he was cursed. Afflicted with Tourette's Syndrome, a neurological disorder that causes him to utter sounds against his will and his body to jerk wildly at times, this successful major-league ballplayer would get down on his knees and ask God to ease his burden.

Eventually, he came to see it as a blessing. A man of faith, he's convinced God has a plan for him. That plan includes spreading hope. Despite a disease that has caused him anguish and embarrassment, Eisenreich believes his triumphs on the ball field inspire other Tourette sufferers, especially children. So he volunteers time to spend with them.

"I tell kids to keep their heads up," says this husband and father of two. "I tell them to keep working towards their dreams because dreams are possible."

Jim Eisenreich accepts his disease, but never gives in to it. He's never let it stop him from fulfilling his dreams and he's never lost his faith.

My steadfast love shall not depart from you, and My covenant of peace shall not be removed, says the Lord. (Isaiah 54:10)

Let go and let God. This I pray. Let go and let God.

Dangerous when wet

In the 1950s, Hollywood created some movie extravaganzas which still linger in our memories. Who can forget the fantastic water ballets and athleticism of Esther Williams?

Whether she was diving from cliffs, boards or gigantic water columns, swimming beneath, around, and through all manner of coral and goldfish bowl furniture, she was ever the quintessential female at home in her water element. She smiled and swam, perfectly, always with grace and style.

Her career began in Hermosa Beach, California, during the Depression when her sister taught her to swim. But it was her mother who bullied and badgered the local city government to install a playground swimming pool in their neighborhood. Little eight-year-old Esther was the first to inaugurate the pool by diving in and swimming its length. "I got out of the pool and everybody applauded." The rest is film history.

We all start our careers somewhere. Is there a young person you could encourage?

Esther was admired by all who saw her. (Esther 2:15)

When the seas are rough, O Lord, keep me afloat.

Tapping tape's popularity

How many household items have a calendar, two books and a Web site dedicated to their use, history and fame? Well, at least one. Duct tape.

It's true. The ubiquitous gray roll has patched leaky pipes and boats and splinted broken bones. Actually, more than a dozen colors are now available and it started out green when it kept munitions dry during World War II. One of the polyethylene-backed cloth adhesive's finest hours came in 1970. It held together a carbon dioxide filter during the successful rescue of the Apollo 13 space crew.

But, manufacturers hesitate to issue a list of uses. One remarked that "the less we know about duct tape holding on car fenders, the happier we are from a liability standpoint."

The creative mind gets its biggest push in times of necessity. So use all the talents and tools God gave you.

A man going on a journey, summoned his slaves and entrusted his property to them; to one he gave five talents, to another two, to another one. (Matthew 25:15)

Help me look with fresh eyes at all the little things around me, Holy Spirit. Let me appreciate them and use them well.

What's in a word?

There is a new phrase making the rounds among the wheelers and dealers of Hollywood's dream factories. Several years ago we were all encouraged to "Do lunch" or "Take a meeting." This quick-speak now includes "Whatever with that."

This new phrase connotes dismissal along with vast world weariness: it indicates that the idea just presented is not only infeasible but that further exposure to the sensibility that came up with it may send the listener into an intractable stupor.

It's so easy to dismiss people with a few words or a look. In the course of one day, try to keep track of the number of tiny put-downs you inflict on others. We may not mean harm, but it certainly does not help. If you disagree, say so. Otherwise — encourage and be kind.

When words are many, transgression is not lacking, but the prudent are restrained in speech. (Proverbs 10:19-20)

Let me be simple without being a simpleton, Holy Spirit.

Making, teaching peace

What can one person do for peace?

At the request of his government Kenyan journalist and lay missionary Joseph Ngala has mediated the release of captives in the Sudan. He also heads three schools for the hearing impaired.

"People for Peace in Africa," an ecumenical group begun by him, won the first Maryknoll Mission Award for its peace-making efforts between warring tribes. His group also began the first counseling center in Africa for victims of violence.

Peace, he says, is a deliberate decision. It's a daily commitment to resolving conflicts and getting along. Peace is finding solutions to seemingly illogical problems. And it's people learning how to talk to and with each other.

And, Ngala says, peace is women teaching men to choose the peaceful over the violent. Women who see the life-long effects of violence on their children.

Joseph Ngala is doing what he can for peace in Kenya and in Africa. What are you doing for peace? Begin *within* yourself.

A harvest of righteousness is sown in peace for those who make peace. (James 3:18)

Prince of Peace, show us how to be peace-filled, peace-makers.

What religions have in common

Father Thomas Keating, a noted leader in worldwide inter-religious dialogue, first met with a diverse group of Buddhist, Tibetan Buddhist, Hindu, Jewish, Islamic, Native American, Russian Orthodox, Protestant and Roman Catholic spiritual teachers in 1984.

"The world religions bear witness to the experience of Ultimate Reality," writes Father Keating. And to it "they give various names: Brahman, Allah, Absolute, God, Great Spirit."

This Ultimate Reality may be experienced not only through religious practices but also through nature, art, human relationships and service to others, notes Father Keating.

The participants shared these things in common: the importance of compassion; fasting and abstinence; the practice of moral precepts and virtues; the use of music, chanting, sacred symbols; pilgrimage and the study of sacred texts.

Differences are familiar; similarities, surprising.

Thus says King Cyrus of Persia: . . . Any of . . . you who are of His people . . . are now permitted to go up to Jerusalem . . and rebuild the house of the Lord. (Ezra 1:2,3)

Inspire us and our religious leaders, God, to unite in respect, peace, love and understanding.

There was no joy on the farm

"Going. Going. Gone!" One by one, 129 dairy cows were sold and loaded into trailers. Standing in the big red-and-white tent, the legendary Lepine sisters watched as their dairy farm disappeared with each bang of the gavel.

Therese, Jeannette and Gertrude Lepine retain the land, but their failing health and encroaching age make it impossible for them to continue. The sisters owned, arguably, the best dairy herd in the state. Years ago, Vermont had 11,000 dairy farms. Today there are fewer than 1,200.

One sister was a stewardess, another was a school teacher and all three returned to the family farm as early as 1952. It was hard work (their hands show the labor), but being in the middle of the Green Mountains with the freedom to ". . . sing when I wanted to and swear when I wanted to," was all that was necessary. When you are doing what you love, even work is joy.

Power belongs to God, and steadfast love belongs to You, O Lord. For You repay to all according to their work. (Psalm 62:11-12)

Work as if everything depended upon you; pray as if everything depended upon God.

Tanning to survive

So you thought a sun tan was something only humans took on!

Amazingly, marine biologist Christopher Lowe and his wife Gwen discovered that a school of hammerhead sharks, when put into a shallow pool in bright sunlight, actully changed color.

Yes, the hammerheads developed tans. And they didn't seem to burn or get skin cancer, unlike other fish in a similar environment, or, of course, people. It appears that browning one's skin is not just fashionable, it's evolutionary.

God's universe works in mysterious ways, even in the underwater kingdom. Man and beast find ways to survive.

With the aid of the Holy Spirit, we thrive.

The Advocate, the Holy Spirit, whom the Father will send in My name, will teach you everything. (John 14:26)

Bless the beasts and the children, Dear Lord.

Mapping the way

Without a map to show the way, it's easy to get lost.

So when Phyllis Pearsall arrived in London in the mid-1930's and found herself relying on an out-of-date map of the city, she channeled her frustration into creating the "London A to Z" map business. The indefatigable Mrs. P. would often walk for 18 hours a day, rising at 5 a.m. to eventually cover some 3,000 miles of London's labyrinth of streets. The maps were an instant success and remain a favorite today.

The "doyenne of maps" never misplaced her sense of humor and humility. Asked once if she ever got lost, she replied, "Always, dear."

Seems that's the way it is for most of us. We lose our way for a time but, thanks to the guidance of the Holy Spirit, we eventually find the right path. It's wise to keep our own internal map close at hand.

"What woman having ten silver coins, if she loses one of them, does not light a lamp, sweep the house, and search carefully until she finds it?" (Luke 15:8)

I once was lost but now am found, thanks to You, dear Lord.

Monkeys see and children do

You can't give what you haven't got. As parents, you must have a firm grip on yourself and your belief system *before* you can instill it, or even expect your children to possess it.

How can you expect those tender minds to filter out negative behavior from positive admonitions?

Ask yourself some questions: Do I send my children to church or do I take them? Do I use alcohol or tobacco while insisting the children "just say no"? Am I more concerned about what they wear than their character? Do I transfer my responsibility to school, church, or state? Am I an example of healthy sexuality and love? Am I involved in any community activities or do I insulate myself from others?

Children can pierce right through hypocrisy. They need example as much or more than they need discipline. Children are our greatest treasure. Let's not waste one.

You are all children of light, and children of the day: we are not of the night, or of darkness. (1 Thessalonians 5:5)

Lord, increase my patience, my courage and my approachability.

Invest in yourself to succeed

Pierre Cossette is making a name for himself on Broadway. The Quebec native does what few other producers on the Great White Way dare. He invests in his own shows.

Rather than depend on the usual practice of having outsiders put up the financing, Cossette does it himself. And he believes that's one of the keys to his success. "The Will Rogers Follies," his first such venture, won the Tony Award for Best Musical. "The Civil War" and "The Scarlet Pimpernel" became his next projects.

The producer, who is also involved with television and films, says success comes from tenacity, dedication and a sense of humor. Risk and competition are givens. Don't fear them. Finally, share your rewards.

Success has its own meaning for each person. Attitudes, beliefs, material and personal desires play a part. Before you can achieve your goals, decide what's important: What's worth the investment of yourself?

Human beings . . . You have made them a little lower than God, and crowned them with glory and honor. (Psalm 8:4,5)

Holy Trinity, I need help in seeing what matters and in realizing my dreams.

The art of food

Babette's Feast, Eat, Drink, Man, Woman and more recently, *Big Night,* are films that examine and exalt the role an elaborately and lovingly prepared meal plays in life. Each is the product of a different nation and culture, lending a universality to the very human desire to bake and break bread with others.

What better way to express love and appreciation of family and friends than to share a pleasing repast? On a loftier level, there are those for whom the kitchen is a canvas, the creation of fine cuisine a painting.

In *Big Night,* a pair of Italian immigrant brothers struggle to make a success of their small restaurant. The older of the two, the chef who labors artistically over his dishes, insists on an idealistic approach to attracting a following: "If you give people time, they learn."

The proof is in the pudding, for later, in the midst of a raucous banquet scene, we watch as the guests bite into their food, then close their eyes in silent and joyous rapture.

Food, food, glorious food!

> **He rained down on them manna to eat, and gave them the grain of heaven. (Psalm 78:24)**

Thank You, Jesus, for the Eucharistic meal.

Support from back home

When American men and women in uniform go overseas they don't lose touch with life back home.

Since 1941 when they started pouring coffee and serving doughnuts, the volunteers of the United Service Organizations (USO) have made sure that soldiers and sailors have a needed time out. Headliners like blues guitarist B. B. King and the rock group Hootie and the Blowfish continue the tradition of entertaining the troops — without pay. Bob Hope performed a remarkable 1,000 shows.

General Carl Mundy, head of the USO and former commandant of the Marine Corps, is also concerned with the day-to-day welfare of military people. "It's family support," he says. So the USO gives them e-mail links to home as well as help making the transition to civilian life.

Everyone needs support from others just to get from one day to the next. Let's make a point of recognizing and returning the favor.

The Lord was my support (Psalm 18:18)

When others put themselves on the line for me, Lord, inspire me to reciprocate or, at least, say "Thanks."

"You never know whom you're raising"

One woman in New York City is using her childhood experience to help out a new breed of parents.

Rolanda Pyle works as the head of the New York City Department of Aging's Grandparents Resource Center. She helps grandparents who are raising their grandchildren because their own parents can't. The reasons vary from a parent's drug abuse to AIDS.

Pyle herself was raised by her grandmother from the age of three. Her grandmother provided a loving, faithful role model that inspired Pyle to work in child welfare.

Pyle provides help and support to these often frustrated and overwhelmed caretakers. "They often feel the children are not grateful," she says. She then shares her own story, and gives examples of celebrities who were raised by grandparents: Oprah Winfrey, Carol Burnett, James Earl Jones. "You never know whom you're raising."

Each one of us can have a positive influence on a child's life.

Grandchildren are the crown of the aged. (Proverbs 17:6)

Help us to be wise and loving parents and grandparents, Father.

What's in a name?

In 1944, Texas Congressman Maury Maverick coined the word "gobbledygook" to mean talk or writing that was long, pompous and vague.

Interestingly enough, Congressman Maverick himself was a coined word — in a manner of speaking. His grandfather, Samuel, was the first "maverick."

The story told is that Samuel Maverick, a lawyer and occasional rancher, failed to brand his calves. It's not clear if this was an oversight or reflected his feelings about cruelty to animals.

Whatever the case, Samuel's neighbors disliked his practice because Maverick claimed as his own all unmarked yearlings. Soon maverick came to mean an unbranded animal.

Eventually, maverick came to mean what it does today, nonconformists who don't follow any group or party.

Words may come and go, or change meanings, but they always matter. Use them with care.

I myself will be shepherd of My sheep. (Ezekiel 34:15)

Lord, God, may I always praise Your holy name.

Consider the "dumb" monkeys

Mom was 22, a good age for a Rhesus monkey. Her last baby, Azalea, was slow, hesitant, clumsy, uncoordinated. She was also very aggressive with older monkeys.

But mom did not reject her.

And her big sister hugged her more often.

Even the monkeys she tried to pick fights with didn't return her hostility. She was simply accepted.

Azalea had an extra chromosome which would have caused retardation had she been human.

No rejection. More frequent hugs. Acceptance "as is." Characteristics of dumb monkeys? Or, worth pondering by humans?

Some humans are born slow, hesitant, uncoordinated, clumsy. Some are aggressive for no reason. Others have obvious handicaps or look different from birth.

Which makes one wonder who is more humane. Dumb monkeys? Or wise humans?

As a mother comforts her child, so I will comfort you. (Isaiah 66:13)

Creator, show us where human actions have contributed to the mental, emotional and developmental handicaps of too many. Then help us eliminate these.

No excuses

Jason Kidd, who has made his mark as a star basketball player, names his dad as his hero — and mentions bowling in the explanation.

"When I was a boy, my father used to take me bowling," Kidd explains, "and I wasn't very good. But I always made excuses why I wasn't good. My father said, 'Quit that. The reason you're not a good bowler is that you don't practice.' And he was right. Now if I have a defect, I work at it. I don't make excuses."

Even today, an hour after every Dallas Mavericks practice ends, Kidd can still be found running up and down the court, stopping and shooting jump shot after jump shot.

A lesson for each of us, on or off the court. Keep practicing.

That (seed) in the good soil, these are the ones who, when they hear the word, hold it fast in an honest and good heart, and bear fruit with patient endurance. (Luke 8:15)

Help me, Father, to always do the best with the talents You have given me.

Listen to your tears

Regardless of whether crying comes easy or hard, most of us never quite know why the waterworks of joy, sorrow or relief have been activated.

Rest assured, when the tears do come, it's best to go with the flow and pay close attention. It could be God speaking to you through the drops, reminding you of who you are and where you come from. And of the heart that humanizes you.

It could be a childhood memory that causes us to cry, or a piece of music, or a work of art or a favorite movie. For many males of a certain age, especially those whose fathers have passed away, the ending of the film *Field of Dreams*, when Kevin Costner's character meets his estranged father as a young man, is especially emotional. Simply recalling having a catch with your own dad can bring on the tears, and provide a cathartic and cleansing moment for even the most macho of men.

Jesus offered up prayers and supplications, with loud cries and tears. (Hebrews 5:7)

Let me not hold back the tears, Saving Lord.

When marriage is spelled 'respect'

Respect for your spouse can spell the difference between marital bliss — and misery.

Married couples agreed on the importance of these respectful behaviors:

- Tell each other how you feel — in words or actions.
- Really listen to each other.
- Give of your time.
- Treat each other with courtesy.

Judith Abbott of Lewisburg, Pennsylvania, notes that a friend was critical of her when she thanked her husband for making the bed. "Big deal," the friend said. "Does he thank you for cooking dinner?" "As a matter of fact," Judith responded, "he does."

All our relationships with spouse, family members, friends, co-workers should be marked with respect. It is the greatest gift you can give someone you care about.

> **Lead a life worthy of the calling to which you have been called, with all humility and gentleness, with patience, bearing with one another . . . maintain(ing) the unity of the Spirit in the bond of peace. (Ephesians 4:1-3)**

Give married couples peace, Jesus.

Loving fathers

Support, strength and sensitivity. These are the qualities that comprise a good father, one who provides a framework for trust and love within a family.

Children cry out for their fathers. Our world is rife with fractured families due to divorce, dysfunction and drugs of all kinds. As God guides His children to walk upright in the world, so does a father provide an example of righteousness for his progeny.

God placed a trust in fathers. Their special responsibility is to be strong in love, yet gentle in guidance; to support the family's needs, and to serve with wisdom, calmness and laughter.

Let's do all we can to give fathers as well as mothers and children the respect and practical support they need to make homes and families filled with love.

The Lord honors a father above his children, and He confirms a mother's right over her children. (Sirach 3:2)

Dear Father, lead families along the path of righteousness.

Your home, your refuge

Here are some easy tips for making your apartment or home more of a refuge for both body and soul.

Exchange street shoes for slippers once inside the front door.

Use lamps, not harsh ceiling lights. You'll also find it easier to read with lamps.

Use candles to set a relaxed mood at dinner several times a week.

Personalize the walls by displaying family members' — or your own — talents. Hang the artist's pictures. Display the collector's collection. Frame and hang vacation pictures, diplomas, awards. Show off trophies.

A house is a residence. A home is where the inhabitants can take refuge. Where they feel welcomed, accepted, encouraged, even celebrated. Make your house a home, whether just for yourself or for you and your family.

Father of orphans and protector of widows is God in His holy habitation. God gives the desolate a home to live in. (Psalm 68:5-6)

Bless our homes with Your "shalom," God.

The bonds of competition

Invented at the Rugby School in England in 1823, rugby is a sport that transcends borders and establishes lifelong bonds between players.

Competitors pride themselves on rugby's camaraderie, derring-do, and postgame enjoyment of ale and song. Players wear next to nothing in the way of protection, and though the games are rough and tumble, seldom do fights occur.

Says New Zealander Scott Pierce, "The players are not getting a cent. They're playing to have a great time and meet people who will be friends forever."

Competing for the sheer fun and comradeship of it. How refreshing in these days of $100 million athletes and tabloid tales of drugs and sex scandals.

Let's not lose sight of the purity of a well-played contest.

A joyful heart is life itself, and rejoicing lengthens one's life span. (Sirach 30:22)

Thank You, God, for the ability to run and leap.

More than sugar and spice

In the 1994 bestseller, *Failing at Fairness: How America's Schools Cheat Girls,* some shocking statistics are sighted about how we penalize girls and women in our society.

The thesis is that we teach girls differently from boys: paying less attention to them in the classroom, offering them less feedback and encouragement in discussions, providing them with fewer role models in textbooks, and actively discouraging them from academic success, particularly in the fields of math and science. If this is true, we are damaging generations of human beings with valuable contributions to make.

When we deprive girls and young women of their own stories, adventures, and dreams, we impoverish their imaginations and rob them of their futures.

Fairness should become second nature to us and increase our development as a human family.

Blessed is she who believed that there would be a fulfillment of what was spoken to her by the Lord. (Luke 1:45)

Help me to see everyone as a reflection of Your goodness, just, merciful and loving Lord.

Breeding pride

In 1877, the Nez Perce Indians, who were famous for the quality of horses they bred, were ordered by the U.S. government to leave eastern Oregon for a small Idaho reservation.

Some 800 Nez Perce and 2,000 of their famous horses fled. Four months and 1,100 miles later, just 30 miles from refuge in Canada, the U.S. Army caught them. Chief Joseph said poignantly, "I will fight no more forever." The Nez Perce's connection with horses was destroyed; the tribe settled in Idaho.

Today, the Nez Perce are resurrecting their horse culture through a selective breeding program. The new breed has been named the Nez Perce horse. Says Randy Shebala, the head of the program, "These horses will help us get our old ways back . . . We want a horse that people will remember us for." Rosa Yearout adds, "The outside of a horse helps the inside of a kid."

God has blessed all peoples and cultures with reasons for pride and self-esteem. To nurture these is to achieve selfhood and potential.

Pay . . . respect to whom respect is due, honor to whom honor is due. (Romans 13:7)

Enable us to respect others' traditions and our own, Lord.

A voice of truth

Red Barber is best remembered as the "voice" of two New York baseball teams — the Brooklyn Dodgers and the New York Yankees.

Those who knew the sportscaster marveled at his ability to make radio fans really "see" what was happening on the field — and they spoke, too, of his honesty.

In calling one televised Yankee game, during a losing streak for the team, Barber asked that the stadium — populated by only a few fans — be shown on camera. Yankee officials refused. So Barber told the fans what they could not see. And that year, the Yankees did not renew Barber's contract.

After Barber's death, Bob Edwards said that the part of his friend and fellow sportscaster he especially loved and admired was that Barber "told the truth — no matter what."

A lesson in a life, and a goal for each of us.

Let us speak the truth to our neighbors. (Ephesians 4:25)

Jesus, for each of us, You alone are the way, the truth and the life.

Meeting a need

Volunteer programs often start with one person who sees a need and does something about it.

Annette Williams of New York City worked to start a volunteer tutoring program at her daughter's school because she learned first-hand about the need for it.

Her daughter's teacher wanted to put the girl in a special education class because she needed some extra help. Mrs. Williams didn't want her daughter taken out of her regular class. So she and other volunteers she organized began tutoring the children who needed more work and attention in some subject.

These volunteers do more than teach children reading or writing or math, for example. They help them build the skills and self-confidence they need to become productive members of the community.

Volunteer. It can change everything, one person at a time.

**You may not withold your help.
(Deuteronomy 22:3)**

Remind us, Good Shepherd, of our obligation to help one another.

The tiniest of creatures

Mavis Righini never met a hedgehog she didn't like.

These diminutive creatures, seldom seen by Americans, are familiar to most of us from the bizarre croquet match described in Lewis Carroll's *Alice in Wonderland.*

However, these adorable little animals are protected and cared for in a South London hospital for sick, injured, orphaned or distressed hedgehogs by Mrs. Righini. A vast catalogue of injuries and diseases haunt these small bristly nocturnal creatures. "They're not overblessed with intelligence," says Anne Jenkins, a spokeswoman for the British Hedgehog Preservation Society, "and they're pretty prickly. Their coat is like a bed of nails."

Despite their problems, the hedgehog population stays rather steady in a country which loves animals almost as much as they love children. You can hold them in your hand, and they roll right into your heart.

Make a point of enjoying the beauty and charm of God's creatures.

I praise You, I am fearfully and wonderfully made. (Psalm 139:14)

Help me to see Your majesty in the smallest creatures, Gentle Father.

The greatest gift of friendship

When former First Lady Bess Wallace Truman was 18, her father committed suicide. The family was distraught and confused. Nothing prepared them for this sudden shock.

The first to comfort Bess Wallace was her next door neighbor and closest friend, Mary Paxton, who had recently lost her mother to tuberculosis. They spent two hours that morning just walking, saying nothing.

Mary Paxton knew that a caring presence, a loving companionship could be as healing as words of comfort. There is no need to speak: often, there is little to say. Just being there is often all that is needed.

Jesus is like that, too. Also present. Never judgmental. Not constantly speaking to you, but nearby with healing, caring, loving. Just by being Himself.

Where can I go from Your Spirit? Or where can I flee from Your Presence? (Psalm 139:7)

Jesus, keep me ever mindful of Your Presence in my life and in the lives of everyone I meet.

Say the magic words

From the outside, Tom Harken's life looked picture perfect. As a child, he battled polio and won. As an adult, he started a restaurant chain that made him millions.

But Harken had a secret. In an acceptance speech for the Horatio Alger Award, given to men and women who have overcome adversity to achieve greatness, Harken revealed that up until recently he had been illiterate.

His childhood illness kept him out of school so much that catching up was difficult. An impatient and cruel teacher didn't help.

With his wife's help — he had confessed the truth to her before their marriage — Harken found ways around his inability to read, but eventually decided to ask for help.

These days, Harken has a new mission in life: "I want people to know that they can go into any library and just say the magic words, 'Will you help me?' and someone will help you learn how to read."

In everything do to others as you would have them do to you. (Matthew 7:12)

Give me the courage, Father, to ask for help, and to trust in Your mercy.

Persistence pays off

Chuck Offenburger wouldn't take "no" for an answer in his quest for a pair of shoes.

The newspaper columnist knew that G. H. Bass and Company of Maine made specialized footwear. They had created the special-order boots worn by aviator Charles Lindbergh as he flew across the Atlantic and by Admiral Richard Byrd on his expeditions to the South Pole. So he asked Bass to replace his worn out but beloved black-and-white saddle shoes with a new pair.

A company executive refused because "we hadn't made men's saddle shoes since 1978." But rather than give up, Offenburger sprang into action using his column in the *Des Moines Register.* He got the support of readers who also cherished the saddle shoe.

With evidence of public interest, Bass agreed to manufacture a limited order, which turned out to be larger than anticipated. Then, buyers attending an industry show signaled their interest as well. The company realized it made sense to put the shoes back into regular production.

Bass is pleased. So is Chuck Offenburger. His example shows us the value of persistence.

Be persistent whether the time is favorable or unfavorable. (2 Timothy 4:2)

Enable us, Lord, to be steadfast.

Return of the buffalo?

The last wild buffalo herd in North Dakota was destroyed around 1875. And the buffalo nearly became extinct in the United States about 100 years ago.

Today, though, the incredible, indestructable buffalo is making a comeback. More and more are found, for instance, on the plains of North Dakota. Their unique suitability for life on the prairie is finally being recognized.

Ranchers also find the buffalo a good deal: they can make as much as $900 on each ranch-raised animal whereas cattle are often sold at a loss.

So more and more buffalo are also turning up on North American dinner plates. Health-conscious diners opt for buffalo meat which, though more expensive than beef, is lower in fat, cholesterol and calories.

Still, America will never again be a place where thundering herds of buffalo can freely roam the great river of grass. It is worth thinking about.

Do not boast about tomorrow, for you do not know what a day may bring. (Proverbs 27:1)

Grant me a sense of wonder when I survey all of Your creation, Maker of buffalo and bumble bees.

Nun named MVP

After Xavier University's basketball season ended, the Most Valuable Player award for the men's team went to Sister Rose Ann Fleming.

Sister Rose Ann didn't dribble or dunk the basketball but she did make a lot of academic assists. In appreciation for her concern, effort and results, the team named her their MVP.

As academic advisor to the athletes, Sister Rose Ann prodded and coached the young men in their studies. And she had the unusual authority to bench a player who missed class.

Some such as Tyrone Hill initially challenged her. He later went on to the pros and still keeps in contact with Sister Rose Ann. But as a freshman, he said he was there to play ball. She replied, "No, you're at Xavier to play basketball *and* to get an education."

Since Sister Rose Ann began, each player has graduated in four years. Just the results expected from an MVP.

**Continue in what you have learned.
(2 Timothy 3:14)**

Help our youth, Jesus, to recognize the value of education.

Lincoln on the declaration

How much does the Declaration of Independence have to do with your life? We may give it high marks in American history, but have its words really affected the generations since the American Revolution?

Abraham Lincoln said it spoke of its belief that "nothing stamped with the Divine image and likeness was sent into the world to be trodden on and degraded . . .

"Now . . . if you have been taught doctrines which conflict with the great landmarks of the Declaration of Independence; if you have listened to suggestions which would take from its grandeur, and mutilate the symmetry of its proportions; if you have been inclined to believe that all men are not created equal in those inalienable rights enumerated by our charter of liberty; let me entreat you to come back . . . to the truths that are in the Declaration of Independence."

In an age that is still not convinced that all people are created equal in sight of the law, the Great Emancipator's words still matter.

God created humankind in his image. (Genesis 1:27)

Divine Lord, help me to see Your image more clearly in each of my brothers, each of my sisters.

Simple surroundings

Ah, simplicity! Here are some thoughts about it.

Your home and office are extensions of yourself. And they affect you, your sense of well-being, your health.

What does your environment say about you? Are you the proverbial pack-rat?

Do you love something? Does it help you in some way? Can you use it? Keep it.

Hate something? Does it have negative or bad memories attached to it? Get rid of it — now!

Make your environment a statement of the real you, the creative you.

Don't be afraid to constantly sift through, get rid of, rearrange, repaint, change what you have, your home, your office. Change even in your external environment is a sign of ongoing interior personal growth.

Keep growing. Keep living. Keep changing.

Do not worry about your life, what you will eat or what you will drink, or about your body, what you will wear . . . your heavenly Father knows that you need all these things. (Matthew 6:25,32)

Help me, Gentle Jesus, to go through life as simply and lightly as possible. And help me see just how little "stuff" is needed.

Cookie break

Phil Rizzuto, the famed shortstop and television broadcaster for the New York Yankees, once stopped midway through a live telecast and started munching on some cookies.

"Got some chocolate-chip cookies here. So don't ask me any questions for a batter or so. All right?"

This amusing incident actually contains a valuable lesson. While many of us are too busy or caught up in our daily routines, Phil Rizzuto remembered to treat himself to something he enjoyed — a cookie break!

Any break is good, but a cookie break is even better. It provides a time to slow down, recharge, and reward ourselves for our hard work. And what could be a better reward than some cookies?

Cookies seem to affect people's dispositions. Whether it's a late night snack with the kids, or with co-workers around the water cooler, the cookie break is the great escape!

Take some time to enjoy one of life's simple pleasures. Invite a friend and take a cookie break.

> **Old men and old women shall again sit in the streets of Jerusalem . . . And the streets of the city shall be full of boys and girls playing. (Zechariah 8:4-5)**

Lord, help us to appreciate time with friends.

Is it still good?

The Christophers have a "Prayer for God's Good Earth" that reads . . .

Father . . .
You looked on all that You made
and saw that it was good.
But we have been too willing
to squander the richness of creation.
We have laid the ax to the mighty forests
despoiled the green hillsides
wasted earth's mineral wealth.
. . . fouled the air
littered the countryside
and polluted the streams and oceans.

Scan a newspaper, newsmagazine or list of newly published books. Watch TV news programs. We seem inured to pollution and destruction. But the consequences for our health, the safety of our food and water, the survival of our planet are alarming.

The prayer continues, ". . . stop us from squandering our patrimony." Yes, stop us, Lord.

Incline your ear, and come to Me, listen, so that you may live. (Isaiah 55:3)

Lord, teach me to listen.

Healing hope

When she was offered the job as the first chaplain in the Burn Center of New York Hospital-Cornell Medical Center, Rev. Carolyn Yard initially said, "No." But then, after a night of prayer, she said, "Why not me?" and told hospital officials she would take the post.

As chaplain, Yard offers burn victims a hug, a simple touch, a greeting, a prayer, a patient ear — hope.

She has also helped those responsible for the burn injuries — including many parents — come to terms with their actions. And she always has time for the staff of the center.

Nurse Richard Thalman says: "What is wonderful about Carolyn is that she goes in the patient's room without an agenda. She goes in there as a human being."

Reflecting on the lesson of her job, Yard offers: "We take life for granted. What would we do differently if we knew that this was our last day?"

Just as you did it to one of the least of these who are members of My family, you did it to Me. (Matthew 25:40)

Give me Your vision, Creator, to see Your image in all persons.

The ways of peace

When two gangs met at a park in California's San Fernando Valley it was to play softball, not fight.

The event was part of a truce of several years standing between deadly enemies, the oldest gangs in the valley, Pacoima and San Fernando. It was arranged through the Valley Unity Peace Treaty, a community group with support from local government and law enforcement agencies.

It has not been easy to keep the terms of the agreement — "no violence, no drive-bys" — on a day-to-day basis among all the gang members. Hence the need for an occasional activity to refocus attention on their efforts. Besides the game, the former rivals shared barbecued chicken, a group photo, and a prayer.

William Rodriquez, a founder of the Valley Unity group who has lost a son to gang violence, opened the event by praying: "Lord, we ask that You continue to give every one of these young men the strength to keep going."

Violence takes a terrible toll. Help your community build peace.

Blessed are the peacemakers, for they will be called children of God. (Matthew 5:9)

Peace makes demands on us all, Lord. Show me how to do my share.

Make the most of today

Anita Septimus, a social worker in New York City, began working with HIV-infected children in 1985. In her first few months she wondered how she could help them. What was the point of working with them if they were only doomed to a young death?

She realized that she had the ability to help these kids and their families make the most of the time they have left. She and her staff look after more than 300 families at the Family Comprehensive AIDS Center. They hope to give these sick children a happy childhood, with trips to the zoo, the circus and summer camps. "She makes us feel wonderful about ourselves," says Petra Berrios, an HIV-positive woman who is also a mother.

"You don't choose the day you enter the world and you don't choose the day you leave," says Septimus. "It's what you do in between that makes all the difference."

Are *you* making all the difference to someone else?

So teach us to count our days that we may gain a wise heart. (Psalm 90:12)

Jesus, who grew in age and wisdom, guide our own growth in wisdom through the years.

Lessons in a life

He lost his job, was publicly humiliated, and his family lived in poverty.

But Chiune Sugihara, a consul for Japan living in Lithuania in the 1930's, did not regret a single action which led to his life's circumstances. It is believed that the more than 2,100 visas he signed for Jews fleeing Eastern Europe and the Nazis helped 8,000 to 10,000 people escape.

Dr. Anne S. Kadish is part of Sugihara's legacy. As a child of Holocaust survivors, she heard often of her family's escape from Poland — and of the "mystical Japanese person" who signed visas for her desperate parents. (Kadish was born three years after their escape.)

"We need to honor and cherish the people who help others all over the world," Kadish said. "We need to teach our children their characteristics and their stories — teach them for us, the survivors . . ."

The integrity of the upright guides them. (Proverbs 11:3)

Give us strength, Father, when doing what we know is right is difficult and sometimes dangerous.

A path to reconciliation

Reminders of America's cruel and tragic history of slavery rarely serve as symbols of reconciliation. But that's what has happened to a Maryland plantation and the families associated with it.

Agnes Callum, 71, a retired postal worker, amateur genealogist and the descendant of slaves, and John Hanson Briscoe, 62, a circuit court judge and the descendant of slave owners, are friends and colleagues on the Sotterley Plantation Board of Directors.

It was Mrs. Callum's research which gave the judge a more complete understanding of the history of his family, who had once owned the plantation and run it with slave labor.

"She has never made me feel ashamed or that I had to say I was sorry," said Judge Briscoe. "It never crossed my mind," said Mrs. Callum. "It was his great-grandfather. I'd be insulted if he apologized. He didn't do anything to me."

Mrs. Callum is pleased they're now both on the board. "We've finally come full circle. We're equals at last."

There is no longer Jew or Greek, there is no longer male and female; for all of you are one in Christ Jesus. (Galatians 3:28)

Inspire us, Lord, to forgive others, and ourselves, and to make amends when necessary.

In praise of God's creation

St. Francis of Assisi lived over 800 years ago, but he is still revered and loved as probably only a handful of other saints are. Part of his appeal lies in his affection for all creation, for all of God's creatures.

Here, he gives us something to think about when looking at the birds of the air:

"Little Brother Bird, who brims with full heart, and having nothing, possesses all, surely you do well to sing! For you have life without labor, and beauty without burden, and riches without care.

"When you wake, lo, it is dawn; and when you come to sleep it is evening. And when your two wings lie folded about your heart, lo, there is rest.

"Therefore sing, Brother, having this great wealth, that when you sing you give your riches to all."

Listen to the songs of the birds with fresh ears, watch them soar with fresh eyes. And be grateful to their Creator and ours.

Look at the birds of the air; they neither sow nor reap nor gather into barns, and yet your heavenly Father feeds them. (Matthew 6:26)

Thank You, Holy Creator and Lord, for the wonder of nature, for our companion creatures in the world.

Jammin' on a Sunday afternoon

Pianist and playwright Marjorie Eliot decided that jazz needed to be rescued from over-priced-two-drink-minimum nightclubs.

Jazz, she says, is "the essence of who African-Americans are." And "with clubs . . . it's not in the hands of people who cherish it — people whose emotional lives depend on it."

She knew that "music at home was just a part of what you did as a cultured person."

So Ms. Eliot opened her living room to free Sunday afternoon jazz gigs. Both musicians and audiences consider it a worthwhile, even wonderful experience. As one of her guests said, "The greatest thing you'll ever learn is just to love."

That's a pretty good idea for each of us. Do something for love, and trust people to love in return. You, your neighbors and your neighborhood will be the better for it.

A ruby seal in a setting of gold is a concert of music at a banquet of wine. A seal of emerald in a rich setting of gold is the melody of music with good wine. (Sirach 32:5-6)

Thank You for the gift of music and for the skill of musicians, Lord of the Dance.

Go fish!

How would you like to spend two hours under water without a wet suit? How would you like to see 500 species of marine life? Or travel all over the globe viewing authentic reproductions of natural marine habitat? You can do all this and remain dry when you visit Europe's largest aquarium in Genoa, Italy.

You can see the Red Sea tropical with 40 species of fish and coral in colorful splendor. Experience the humidity of the Amazon rain forest where reptiles and snakes await their next meal from steamy waters. Wonder at dolphins, sharks, penguins, and giant turtles from the Maldives. See all manner of endangered sea life in comfort.

The aquarium also works closely with marine conservationists to protect and preserve species. Genoese school children and visitors are touched by the marvel and mystery of God's undersea creation even as they learn responsible stewardship for the oceans, the Earth.

Wonder ideally leads to stewardship.

> **God created the great sea monsters and every living creature . . . with which the waters swarm. (Genesis 1:21)**

> *All praise and glory be to You, O God, for the infinite variety and beauty of Your creation.*

With God at her side . . .

Walking down the aisle may be a big step figuratively speaking, but for Wendy Petzold, it was, literally, a tremendous step.

Her legs were paralyzed in an auto accident when she was 17. For her to walk down the aisle on her wedding day, using braces and a walker, required a year of intensive physical therapy.

Ms. Petzold sees her disability as a challenge. She didn't let it prevent her from finishing high school and going on to college. Or from playing tennis and ice hockey in her wheelchair or from swimming, scuba diving, and driving a car. Her determination encourages others with disabilities.

She says, "Between God and me, there's nothing we can't face together."

A positive outlook can accomplish wonders.

> **If God so clothes the grass of the field . . . will he not much more clothe you . . . ? (Matthew 6:28-30)**

Merciful Savior, clothe us with trust in Your providential care.

Health for the whole person

Bernie Siegel, M.D., believes good health is more than physical well-being.

"Stress, despair and hopelessness weaken our bodies just as hope, joy and love sustain them," writes Dr. Siegel. "Emotions communicate with our immune system and other organs via neuropeptides."

Using questions developed by psychiatrist George Solomon to test for an "immune competent personality," Dr. Siegel focuses attention on ways body, mind and spirit work together.

The questions to ask include: Do I have a sense of meaning in my work, daily activities, family and relationships? Am I able to express anger appropriately in defense of myself? Am I able to ask friends and family for support and to request favors when needed?

Also, are you able to do good things for yourself? Are you able to play?

Body, mind and spirit work together for good health.

Health and fitness are better than any gold, and a robust body than countless riches. (Sirach 30:15)

Father, bless our efforts to become whole and healthy in body, mind and soul.

Change attitudes, offer forgiveness

Three pastors are working to heal a town in the aftermath of a terrible bias crime.

Citizens of Fayetteville, North Carolina, were shocked and pained when three white soldiers from nearby Fort Bragg were arrested for murdering two young African-Americans. Racial tension gripped the town.

Pastor Larry Jackson refuses to curse the darkness — he's gotten hundreds of people who live in Fayetteville to light candles in their windows as a sign of hope. His goal, a candle in every window of the town.

Pastors Lee Downing and Michael Fletcher organized a service to help the residents address their pain and fear. Over 800 people attended.

At the religious service, the aunt of one of the victims spoke of forgiving the soldiers. "When those who were the most injured talked about forgiveness," said pastor Downing, "that was the impetus for reconciliation."

Forgiveness *is* the first step to healing.

> **If one has no mercy toward another like himself, can he then seek pardon for his own sins? (Sirach 28:4)**

Remind us, Holy Spirit, that violence breeds violence; forgiveness, peace.

Is the grass greener?

Rural living was supposed to be an idyllic change from the stress and grime of the city. It was supposed to offer scenic beauty unavailable even in the suburbs. So Francine Prose, her husband and their two young sons moved 100 miles away from Manhattan.

The boys' grade school was terrific, staffed by caring and dedicated teachers. But things deteriorated when the children entered junior high. Some teachers were complacent and a few were cruel. Creativity and excellence were not appreciated. The school wasn't immune from drugs, violence and overcrowded classes.

"Gradually our placid country life lost its appeal," wrote Ms. Prose. "Our sons had little to do and nowhere to go . . . (and) I had never stopped missing the buzz of city life."

The family returned to New York. Rather than thinking the grass is greener somewhere else, it might be wiser to more fully appreciate where you are and how you can improve it for the better.

The cities shall be for you a refuge. (Numbers 35:12)

Help us to develop a greater appreciation for what's important in our lives, Lord.

Say two prayers and call me . . .

Dr. Randolph Byrd divided 393 coronary care unit patients at San Francisco General Hospital into two groups. The first names of the patients in one group were given to prayer groups. The other group of patients wasn't remembered in prayer. When the study was completed, the prayed-for patients were:

- five times less likely than the unremembered group to require antibiotics.
- 2½ times less likely to suffer congestive heart failure.
- less likely to suffer cardiac arrest.

No doctor today is suggesting that prayer be substituted for modern medical procedures and medicines. But studies do suggest that prayer can lower high blood pressure and anxiety; speed healing; and sooth headaches.

The bottom line: Prayer can be healthful, since it reminds us that we are not alone.

> **Are any among you suffering? They should pray . . . sick? . . . call for the elders of the church and have them pray over them, anointing them. (James 5:13,14)**

> *We thank You, Father, for the gift of prayer. We are confident that You hear our silent and spoken prayers.*

More than a friend

Friends trust each other with very personal things: secrets, confidences, joys and sorrows. Sue Perhus trusted her best friend, Joanne Hazel, with more than just a secret.

Sue and Joanne met when both were 18-year-old roommates in nursing school. Sue was maid of honor when Joanne married. Four years later, Joanne stood up for Sue. Joanne began her family, and Sue, unable to have children of her own, adopted a little girl from Nicaragua.

The two lived 15 miles apart and touched base regularly. A series of tragedies hit Joanne: her husband died, her mother passed away. Both Joanne and her two daughters were reeling from this double sorrow. Suddenly, Sue was killed in an automobile accident.

In her will, Sue had appointed Joanne executor and asked that she be the guardian of her daughter, Erika. Could Joanne and her daughters honor such a request?

It was hard for all four of them. But they made it work. Today, Joanne calls all three young women "my girls."

A friend loves at all times. (Proverbs 17:17)

Help me meet the demands of friendship with generosity and courage.

Who is that long-haired lady?

How do you feel when someone forgets your name? Confuses you with another? That's what happened to Mary Magdalene. Here's what we know:

1. She really lived.
2. She followed Jesus in His public ministry.
3. Jesus cured her of some serious illness (attributed to "seven devils" in her day).
4. She loved Jesus enough to stand by Him at His worst hour.
5. She was the first to see her risen Savior and announce the news to the Apostles.

Whether or not she was related to Lazarus, washed the Lord's feet with her tears and dried them with her hair, or repented from a life of prostitution — or was it one of several other women named Mary? — we may never know for sure.

Love is all that matters. All that is necessary. It made Mary Magdalene a fully realized human being, a saint. Love can do the same for us.

Many women were also there . . . they had followed Jesus from Galilee . . . Among them were Mary Magdalene . . . (Matthew 27:55)

Never let what others think of me keep me from You, Jesus.

For the sake of our children

Grammy Award-winning singer and mother of two, Tramaine Hawkins has always tried to reach teenagers through her music and through personal encounters.

Whenever Hawkins saw kids trying to sell drugs, she would say, "Sweetheart, what's your name? I can't believe you're out here selling this stuff . . . Shame on you! Your parents wouldn't want you to do that. I don't want you to do that."

"Whether it had any lasting effect, I don't know," says Hawkins, "but at least I let them know my feelings, let them know that I was concerned enough about them to say something. We need to wake up and realize the importance of being surrogate parents for some of the young people around us. There is no reason why we can't be mothers and fathers to these kids whose families are not there for them."

Helping young people can change their lives — and our world — forever. Do all you can.

Train children in the right way, and when old, they will not stray. (Proverbs 22:6)

Father, help us guide and cherish all children, just like you do.

Observe — and learn

How often do we settle for just getting through the day without really noticing what's occurring right in front of us? Interesting things happen when we develop our powers of observation.

Keen observers are essential in such fields as literature, journalism, psychology, science, business and administration.

It's also helpful in interpersonal relationships to understand others, their needs and wants.

We may fail to be observant as adults, but it's likely we started out as exquisitely observant children. Youngsters are particularly aware of the behavior of their parents.

To sharpen observational skills, consider the technique of best-selling author W. Somerset Maugham. He always carried a notebook and wrote down even the smallest details about the people and places he encountered. His fiction was celebrated for its ring of truth and emotional insight.

For the observant, life is never boring.

Observe carefully what is before you. (Proverbs 23:1)

Make it possible for us to see the beauty in people and in nature, Almighty God.

African-American accomplishments

African-Americans have a long and distinguished if not always recognized or appreciated history in the United States.

The Black Heritage stamp series highlights some of the most promiment and talented men and women and their contributions to society.

■ Harriet Tubman, abolitionist.

■ Rev. Dr. Martin Luther King Jr., Nobel Peace Prize winner, civil rights activist.

■ Jackie Robinson, major League baseball player.

■ Scott Joplin, composer and pianist.

■ A. Philip Randolph, civil and labor rights leader.

■ Jan Matzeliger, industrial inventor.

■ Bessie Coleman, aviation pioneer.

"Stamps are a very effective way of communicating information," says John Sawyer, a member of the Citizen Stamp Advisory Committee.

Learn about the history and heritage of your own family and the rest of God's people.

Serve one another with whatever gift each of you has received. (1 Peter 4:10)

Jesus, what more can I do to respect and honor others?

Attention mall shoppers: thank Gruen

Anyone who has wandered around an indoor shopping mall should stop to give thanks for this convenient method of shopping.

But who to thank? With Hitler's invasion of Austria in 1938, architect Victor Gruen fled his homeland for America. He brought with him just $8 in his pocket and an idea for a covered shopping mall based on medieval market towns.

His vision became concrete, stone, brick and steel in the mid-1950s when Gruen was commissioned to build a shopping center in Minnesota. He constructed a central courtyard equidistant from two department stores. Its one giant roof meant that construction costs for individual stores could be reduced, making the whole complex cheaper to build.

Soon a new generation of developers was building on Gruen's ideas. Don't be afraid to build on the good ideas of others — and let others build on yours.

Make me to know Your ways, O Lord; teach me Your paths. (Psalm 25:4-5)

Your hand is in everything, Lord. Only with Your help can we realize our dreams, our goals.

Some friendly advice

Actor Charles Grodin became interested in the nature of friendliness after often being told his friendly demeanor was unusual.

He found many people routinely accept unfriendly behavior in their daily lives. Disturbed, he enlisted comedienne Carol Burnett and began a national "friendly" campaign. They used their television resources and fame to raise national awareness of the importance of friendliness. Thousands responded enthusiastically.

Everyone wants to be treated well but we sometimes forget that others want the same thing. Practice these friendly habits:

■ Pause and ask yourself, "How would I like to be treated in this situation?" Simple, but it works.

■ Be the first to be friendly. A simple smile can start a "friendly" chain reaction.

■ Remember, being friendly is its own reward. It makes you and everyone around you feel good.

Value friendliness and encourage others.

Pleasant speech multiplies friends. (Sirach 6:5)

You are my dearest Friend, Jesus. Help me treat others as I would treat You.

Dealing with God's short leash

Former news anchorman and commentator John Chancellor looked forward to a comfortable and relaxing retirement.

Then he found out he had stomach cancer.

At first came the feelings of guilt, with Chancellor asking himsef: "Had I smoked or drunk too much? Exercised or prayed enough?" Next, came the inevitable question: "Why me? After all, cancer didn't run in my family."

Chancellor faced chemotherapy and its dreadful side effects with a sense of humor and the help of his best friend, his wife, Barbara.

How did he see his illness? "Cancer," he explained, "is a reminder of how short a leash you're on." Life is short and it takes unexpected turns. Live as fully and joyously as you can.

Father, into Your hands I commend my spirit. (Luke 23:46)

I am Yours, Lord. I pray that You will love, protect and shelter me as You will.

Gambling's dangerous lure

The addiction of gambling is on the rise. The increase of legalized gambling has made access to betting of one form or another easier.

Here are some trouble signs. If someone has even half of them, professional assistance or a self-help group like Gamblers Anonymous is needed before a life or a whole family is destroyed:

- Preoccupation with gambling
- Increases wager to increase excitement
- Past unsuccessful attempts to stop gambling
- Irritability when not able to gamble
- Gambling used as escape from problems
- Efforts to "get even" after losing by gambling
- Lying to hide gambling involvement
- Committing crimes to get gambling money
- Jobs and relationships put at jeopardy by gambling
- Asking others to cover gambling losses

If you recognize yourself, you are not alone. Call for help now.

Stand firm in your faith. Be courageous. (1 Corinthians 16:13)

God, supply the courage I do not feel to do what I need to do.

It's time to celebrate

Everyone enjoys a celebration. Our ancestors were no exception. Maybe that's why they observed so many different feast days. These also erased overburdened lives filled with monotonous daily labor.

Some of these bygone feasts and their celebration might seem strange. But there's usually an intriguing story about the holiday's development.

Twelfth Night, or January 5th, was a time of high revelry. Before becoming associated with Epiphany, it was a pagan ritual to improve chances for a good grain harvest.

Walpurgisnacht on April 30 was meant to keep the wandering demons loosed by witches' spells at bay. Church bells sounded in the middle of the night. People screamed while banging pots and pans. Bonfires were lighted in the fields.

On *Lammas Day*, August 1st, loaves of bread and sheaves of corn were brought to church as people thanked God for a good harvest.

These feasts brought family and friends together, marked the passage of time, and often offered thanks or asked for protection. Not so different today, is it?

Celebrate your festivals. (Nahum 1:15)

Holy Spirit, assist my efforts to find joy and happiness in the simple pleasures of everyday life.

The big picture

During a conversation among young people in New York City, a study was mentioned that cited a connection between prayer and the improvement of critically ill patients. Both Willie, a student, and Bill, a police officer, expressed a belief in prayer's ability to heal.

Willie said, "I'm not really sure what it all means, but I know that when I pray, regularly, I feel better. I'm not sure about physically, but . . . I can't explain it. I feel happier."

"It's a sense of peace," Bill explained. "That's what it gives you. For people who pray, no matter what else goes wrong in their lives, they always have God. There's less worry and stress because they feel better about the big picture."

"That's probably the answer," concluded Willie. "Maybe God answers prayers about health by keeping you happy through prayer. There's a connection between your mental and physical health, so if praying keeps you relaxed, you'll feel better overall."

What do you think?

At this moment he is praying. (Acts 9:11)

Lord, teach me to pray as You did.

In your own words

My Beloved,

I'd like to hear from you in your words more often.

Confide in Me. Cry on My shoulder. Tell Me when you're blue. Or angry at someone you can't be angry with — you know what I mean. Or achingly lonely. Ask Me for a hug. No strings are attached to Mine.

When life gives you "boo-boos" run to Me. I'll make them all better. When you ache or are sick or concerned about test results, let Me know. At least I'll give you My strength.

Pray for the people in the newspaper or on TV. Especially the violent ones who sow discord, hate, war, bigotry, ignorance.

I like to hear your honest emotions. I won't grade you, honest.

If you need to yell and scream at Me, go ahead.

All I ask is that you talk to Me in your own words.

Your Lord and Lover,
God

Hear my prayer, O God. (Psalm 54:2)

God, give me the courageous wisdom to pray to You.

Live, learn and pass it on

"Thanks coach, but my work is not done here in the South Bronx," Tommy Yahn told Joe Paterno. Penn State University's celebrated football coach had asked Yahn to return to the university and assist with the team.

The "work" the one-time NFL running back was referring to is that of basketball coach to boys and girls in a poor neighborhood. He's not only a coach but a friend, a father figure, and most importantly, an example to the youngsters. Having come from the same area, he is proof that they can rise above difficulties and do well.

Tommy Yahn doesn't measure his success by dollars and cents but by how well he fills this role. "What I do now is invaluable as compared to the money I once made playing pro football."

He owes this outlook to his father, now deceased, who encouraged him and taught him to pursue his dreams. "I wanted to do for these kids what my father had always done for me."

Inspiration is a gift to be handed down from generation to generation.

Teach them the good way in which they should walk. (2 Chronicles 6:27)

Lord of Hope, may I bring Your Good News to all those around me.

Lost — or found? — in the translation

National Geographic magazine ran an interesting article about translating the titles of articles from English into Japanese.

One story was about our resourceful, beady-eyed, bushy-tailed, nut-burying, tree-limb aerialist neighbors.

"In Praise of Squirrels" became the lyrical "Little Lives Darting About the Garden: The True Colors of the Cheery Squirrels."

Another story was memorable for its exquisite if vertiginous photographs, its sure-footed, bearded and horned subjects and their gamboling kids.

That one, "Mountain Goats: On the Edge of Earth and Sky," became the poetic, "White Dancers Living on Cliffs."

The cliché response would be that something becomes lost in the translation. Not with these titles.

And not in our listening if done with care and attention. You can hear the poetic, the lyric, even the tragic, within and underneath the words.

Love enough to listen carefully, attentively.

**Let anyone with ears to hear listen!
(Mark 4:9)**

Open my entire being and my mind to listen long and lovingly for and to You, Spirit of God.

Marathon man

Jerry Dunn is a man who plans on being in it for the long run.

The South Dakotan ran the course of the Boston Marathon every day for 25 days preceding the actual event — making the race itself his 26th 26.2 mile run in 26 days. Before that, Dunn held the world record for running the most marathons in a year, 104.

What possessed this man to push himself to the extreme limit? "I just turned 50," said Dunn. "I want to make a statement about health and fitness in the second half of my life."

That's quite a statement!

You don't have to set world records to live healthily. But you should do your best to maintain a sense of well-being, to be in your best shape — physically, emotionally, mentally and spiritually.

Those who wait for the Lord shall renew their strength, they shall mount up with wings like eagles, they shall run and not be weary, they shall walk and not faint. (Isaiah 40:31)

Lord, help us keep our bodies and souls healthy.

Making a good impression

"When you're trying to resolve a conflict face to face, tell all parties to act as they would if the discussions were videotaped."

This advice comes from Dallas psychotherapist and counselor Susan Sturdivant. Maybe this sounds like a superficial approach, but it seems likely to work. When we're being videotaped or photographed, we want to be seen at our best. And in conflicts we're often at our worst. We get angry and make belittling remarks — attacking the other person instead of dealing with the problem.

Trying to make a good impression may not be the noblest motive, but it can have a positive effect. Being courteous and pleasant to those who disagree with helps resolve problems.

Put away from you all bitterness and wrath and anger and wrangling and slander, together with all malice. (Ephesians 4:31)

Teach us to disagree without being disagreeable, Holy Spirit.

A song for self-esteem

When Dr. Walter J. Turnbull founded The Boys Choir of Harlem in 1970, he wanted to provide an opportunity for youngsters to build self-esteem through music. He had no idea it would grow into the internationally recognized organization it is today.

Self-discipline is the score the young singers follow. "To sing the range they do requires discipline," says Dr. Turnbull, "and that discipline is transferrable to everything else they do."

Small wonder that each year 2,000 youngsters audition to join one of the various choirs. "We're more than a choir," asserts Dr. Turnbull. "We're an institution that's dedicated to helping children be successful."

Let's all sing a tune of self-esteem, even if we go off-key once in a while.

Whose offspring are worthy of honor? Human offspring. Whose offspring are worthy of honor? Those who fear the Lord. (Sirach 10:19)

Let me sing my song of life, Lord of my life.

When doctors speak our language

When it comes to building rapport, it helps to have someone who speaks our language. One of the areas in which this is most important is in the doctor-patient relationship.

Dr. David Baines, a Native American from Alaska, practices near a reservation in Idaho. Because he understands the culture, he doesn't dismiss tribal remedies offhand. He can also help patients deal with fears about Western medicine. For instance, he might persuade a diabetic about the value of taking insulin regularly. "Sometimes they think if you have to keep taking it, it must not be working."

A special fellowship offered by The National Medical Fellowships enabled Dr. Baines to study medicine. When these physicians return to their communities, they often bring a special sensitivity. As the president of that group put it, "They use the same language, literally and figuratively."

There may come a time when recovery lies in the hands of physicians, for they too pray to the Lord that He grant them success in diagnosis and in healing, for the sake of preserving life. (Sirach 38:13-14)

Help us, Holy Spirit, to grow in understanding of others.

Commandments for parents

Parenting *is* a difficult job. Solomonic wisdom and the proverbial "patience of Job" are required.

But some commandments for parents can make this difficult job easier.

● Thou shalt not damage thy children's self-esteem. Ever.

● Be neither under-involved — it makes children feel unlovable and incapable — nor over-involved — it makes children feel pressured and stupid — in thy children's lives.

● Thou shalt listen to thy children, their feelings. Try to understand them. Express your own, too.

● Thou shalt not compare thy children to anyone else, siblings, relatives or others.

● Thou shalt not preach a double standard. What is not acceptable for your children is not acceptable for you either.

God created parents to nurture the spiritual, emotional, intellectual and physical gifts given to each human being born into this world.

The Lord honors a father above his children . . . a mother's right over her children. (Sirach 3:2)

Remind parents of their awesome responsibility to be life-affirming guardians of the children You've given them, Abba.

What to do with a million dollars?

How would you spend a million dollars?

One day the residents of Roby in West Texas were struggling to make ends meet. The next day many were new lottery millionaires. Since then, they've wondered how to answer the question.

Here's what 61-year-old cotton farmer Gene Terry had to sy about his good fortune: "Now I know how I'll be able to make my land payments and my tractor payments." He noted "the pressure's been taken off."

Of the approximately 616 town residents, 39 won the lottery becoming instantly wealthy on their $10 worth of Quik Pick tickets. After taxes, winnings will amount to about $41,000 per winner annually for 20 years. It was all part of a spur-of-the-moment pool at the local cotton gin.

"This is something totally unexpected and just in time," said Manual Valdez. He and his wife Susie "were really struggling with our restaurant."

It's interesting to ponder. How would you spend a windfall? What things do you most value?

The Lord's . . . favor brings lasting success. (Sirach 11:17)

Father, instruct us in Your ways so that we'll know what is truly valuable in life.

Importance of traditions

Did you know that there are over 3,000 state, county and regional fairs in the U.S. and Canada? You would look far to find one more cherished than the Iowa State Fair. Call it an annual time machine back to a slower-paced, quieter America, an 11-day summer celebration, reunion and tradition.

The fair runs in Norma Lyon's blood. Her uncle wrote the novel *State Fair.*

Since 1960, no Iowa fair has been complete without the popular "butter cow" sculptured by Mrs. Lyon. This self-described "Iowa farm wife" puts her all into her bovine creation, along with lots of butter, 550 pounds worth this past year.

Small wonder the cow is in a class by itself and Mrs. Lyon is treated like a queen by the people who cherish her butter figures.

It's the simple and fun things in life that bind us and build our traditions. Let's not lose sight of them.

Rejoice always! (1 Thessalonians 5:16)

God, imbue me with the spirit and fun of celebration.

Little League origins

The Little League is a huge organization. It's made up of more than 2.5 million preteen youngsters in about 11,000 leagues throughout the world. But it all started with one man.

Carl Stotz of Williamsport, Pennsylvania, just wanted to give his two young nephews and other neighborhood boys a chance to have fun playing baseball. He bought "uniforms" at the five-and-ten and supervised their sandlot games. This was in 1939. The idea caught on and the number of leagues grew. Eight years later he organized a World Series between all-star teams in Pennsylvania.

The number of leagues continued to multiply, and in 1974 girls also began playing on teams. The Little League World Series is still held in Williamsport every year.

Many worthwhile organizations begin with one person who takes positive action.

Live lives that are self-controlled, upright, and godly. (Titus 2:12)

Show us how to model our lives on Your life of communion with God in prayer, good deeds and fidelity to the two great Commandments, Jesus.

On the beach with the Shell Lady

Carol Lystad, a.k.a. "The Shell Lady," combs Florida's coast uncovering tiny marine life which others might easily overlook. Her patience, knowledge and obvious delight encourages in others a new appreciation for these gems of the sea.

Over time, the 58-year-old woman's full time love of sea life evolved into part time work as guide. She can pick up sea shells, name them and discuss their unique qualities. As such she is much in demand among vacationers as well as residents.

Ms. Lystad seems to enjoy teaching the young, in particular, calling them "the environmentalists of the future."

When it comes to the environment, she has good news. "I can definitely see improvement on these beaches over the last 25 years. . . . I think people are becoming more sensitive to the need to preserve and protect."

We're more likely to care for things we appreciate.

Where your treasure is, there your heart will be also. (Matthew 6:21)

Creator, show us how to be good stewards of the Earth.

Soup and soul mates

"I recommend to all women looking for a husband to go to a soup kitchen," says Dr. Lisa Tumey, with a smile.

A native of North Carolina, she was completing her residency in pediatrics at a New York hospital and looking to serve in a weekend outreach program. Meanwhile, Dr. Daniel Benz, an internist specializing in the care of AIDS patients, was volunteering his time at a south Bronx soup kitchen and entertaining thoughts of missionary work.

As the doctors see it, the hand of God was evident in their meeting. So was Mother Teresa, whom Dan had met when she visited the Bronx. He confided his struggles with the direction in his life to her and she told him to pray for healing. Three weeks later, early one Saturday morning, Dan met Lisa at the soup kitchen.

These two healers are the picture of a happy and contented couple. Moreover, says Dr. Lisa Benz, "We will always be Catholic physicians and do everything according to the principles of the Church."

Honor physicians for their services for the Lord created them; for the gift of healing comes from the Most High. (Sirach 38:1-2)

Lord, help me live by the courage of my convictions.

Reality check

Are you or someone you know addicted to "clicking and dragging"? Is the World Wide Web now your whole wide world?

Perhaps it's time to turn off the computer and come back to the real world. A. J. Jacobs is the author of "American Off-Line," a helpful guide for Internet addicts who are ready to stop surfing the Web and want to return to reality. In the book, Jacobs offers tips on the non-computerized equivalents of everything from word processing (pencils) to chat rooms (parties).

Modern technology has given us great advantages to help speed work, educate people and entertain. Many talented people have been able to use their God-given gifts to make products that make it easier for others. But there comes a time to draw the line when we lose the human aspect, and forget to interact with others.

Surround yourself with the warmth and love of family and friends, not just the impersonal computer.

The Lord gave skill to human beings that He might be glorified in His marvelous works. (Sirach 38:4,6)

Encourage me to share my gifts and talents with those around me, Creator.

Mechthild (or Machtild) of Magdeburg, a saintly medieval German lay woman, left a list of suggestions on how to behave in various circumstances. Much of it is still relevant.

■ When you pray, you should make yourself small in great humility.

■ When you eat, you should be restrained.

■ When you are alone, you should be faithful.

■ When you are in company, you should be wise.

■ When someone teaches you good habits, you should be attentive.

■ When someone rebukes you, you should be patient.

■ When you do something wrong, then you should immediately seek grace.

■ When you are troubled, then you should have great trust in God.

■ When you work with your hands, you should do so swiftly.

Try to live one of Mechthild's suggestions for a day. Light a candle.

We are God's servants. (1 Corinthians 3:9)

Refresh my optimism, Jesus.

A degree of education

How do you know whether or not you're educated? Here's a quiz from a Chicago professor to help you find out. A "yes" answer to every question indicates that you're educated.

■ Are you sympathetic to and support good causes?

■ Are you public-spirited?

■ Are you a friend to the weak?

■ Can you make friends and keep them?

■ Can you look an honest person in the eye?

■ Is there anything to love in a small child?

■ Are you in a relationship with your Maker?

■ Can you see beyond the stars in the night sky?

■ Can you be optimistic amid life's drudgeries?

No matter how educated you are, your education is never complete. Keep striving to be all that God made you.

The knowledge of the wise will increase like a flood, and their counsel like a life-giving spring. (Sirach 21:13)

Teacher and Lord, help us to keep learning and growing.

Youngsters pray for others' needs

It isn't unusual for parents and religious leaders to encourage children to pray. But letting youngsters handle their own telephone Prayer Line is.

"The idea was to get them into the habit of praying for others," says Sunday school teacher Lisa Schnedler. They set up a number and answering machine. At the beginning of each class the children, aged 6 to 12, listen to the messages. Then they include the requests in their prayers.

People often leave follow-up messages to let the youngsters know how things are. Mrs. Schnedler admits that "the kids were a bit shocked by some of the outcomes, but now they feel that they play a vital role, even if God's answers are not the ones we want."

Prayer matters in ways we may never fully appreciate. Next time you pray for yourself, add one for a loved one; for someone you hardly know.

Father, hallowed be Your name. Your kingdom come. Give us each day our daily bread. And forgive us our sins, for we ourselves forgive everyone indebted to us. (Luke 11:2-4)

You love me so much, God. I'm sorry I don't spend as much time with You as I could. Remember us, Your children.

Giving it your all

Arnold Palmer began golfing at the age of three. Of course, with a dad who was a golf teacher, how could he not have been drawn to the game?

But his father's greatest lesson about golf had little to do with technique, but more with attitude.

The first golfer to win the Masters tournament four times, Palmer recalls: "My father always said to me, 'Remember, whatever game you play, 90 percent of success is from the shoulders up.'"

"You don't have to be the biggest and the strongest," Palmer added. "Your dedication has to be 100 percent. It won't happen if you're doing it because someone said you ought to. You have to have that burning desire. . . . Everything you do has to contribute to the goal, right down to the people you associate with."

That's a good "how to" for life on the course and off.

> **Jesus answered . . . "For this I was born, and for this I came into the world, to testify to the truth. Everyone who belongs to the truth listens to My voice." (John 18:37)**

> *No matter what, help me to always see You, Father, as the center of my life.*

There's always a way to fulfill your dreams

Monika Klein had several dreams.

She had "always wanted to do something that involved horses." And the former CEO wanted to leave the corporate fast track while continuing to use her managerial skills. She also wanted to spend more time with her children.

Once she discovered that her home county had 8,500 horses at last survey she researched owners' unmet needs.

Now Ms. Klein provides experienced temps, herself included, for a variety of horse and barn related chores including horse-sitting. Hence the name of her company, "Horse-Keepers." She runs it from her home office.

She also provides record management services for her clients. And she looks forward to organizing a training program for horses and riders.

Monika Klein used her skills and training to fulfill her dreams.

We can each do the same even if more simply. Dreams fulfilled are the stuff of a happy life.

Listen to this dream that I dreamed. (Genesis 37:6)

Inspire us to dream of and work for an end to all stereotyping and prejudice, Lord God.

Tips from Rover!

If you think about it — and look hard enough — you can learn many important life-lessons from your (or your neighbor's) dog!

Little life-lessons like, walk and nap frequently. And drink plenty of water, too.

Never bite the hand that feeds you or the one that signs your salary checks either.

Don't let anyone make you dress up.

Stop to smell the proverbial roses. And to look at and enjoy everything around you.

Make friends with all your neighbors. Even, maybe especially, the grumps and grouches.

Make those you love feel welcome.

Exercise your body and soul by smiling and laughing frequently.

Once in a while even romp in the freshly fallen snow. Smell the air. Perk up your ears and listen to the muffled silence.

Life is for being, enjoying, growing into a loving person. Make this your priority.

Increase and abound in love for one another and for all. (1 Thessalonians 3:12)

Jesus who delighted in the lilies of the field and the lambs and ewes of the pasture, help us take increasing delight in each person, each creature, each moment, each day.

Meet Mother Necessity

What do Whitcomb L. Judson and Humphrey O'Sullivan have in common? Their feet led them to creativity.

Judson invented the "Clasp Locker and Unlocker," now known as "the zipper" to speed up the process of buttoning and unbuttoning shoes.

Sullivan, after walking about Boston in search of a job, invented the rubber heel to cushion his aching feet.

What these two men really shared was the gift of vision, being able to see beyond difficulty and find opportunity. They learned that inspiration is where you find it.

We have been endowed with the ability and the creativity to overcome obstacles. The hard part is motivating ourselves to use our talents. Henry Kaiser, an American entrepreneur, wrote, "I always view problems as opportunities in work clothes."

Look at everyday difficulties as hidden possibilities waiting to be discovered.

Overcome evil with good. (Romans 12:21)

Lord, may I find inspiration in all You put before me.

When your children are grown-ups . . .

When his view on an issue would differ from that of his young child's, a father of three would often state: "This isn't a democracy; it's a family."

But what happens when sending your child to his or her room is no longer a viable option? How do you have a happy, healthy relationship with grown-up children? Family-issue writer Jane Adams offers parents these tips.

● *Realize that change is necessary.* It's time for a new way of relating to one another — *as friends.* Focus on what you have in common. Treat your children as equals, and know when to back off.

● *Make peace with your children.* This is the time to make amends. Leave their failings and your own in the past.

● *Let grown children make their own mistakes — and have their own dreams.* Maintain the stance that you're always there to help, but be confident that they can make it on their own. Never say, "I told you so." Ask what their goals are — and talk about *their* plans to achieve those goals.

I know the plans I have for you . . . plans for your welfare and not for harm, to give you a future with hope. (Jeremiah 29:11)

Help us to honor You, Father.

Enjoy the season

Summertime, and the living is easy. At least it used to be for most of us — when we were kids. School let out, and we could be carefree. It was a time for kicking back and sleeping late, for swimming, sunning and stone-skipping, not studying.

As adults and parents, it's not that easy to let go and enjoy the season's relaxed rhythms.

But we can encourage our children to enjoy doing some everyday things differently. Then, by sharing many of their activities with them — even if it's just staying up late watching old movies, playing a game of Monopoly, or taking walks along an ocean beach — busy parents might gain anew the true sense of seeing, hearing and feeling.

So put the brakes on and slow down. Enjoy a ray of sunshine and a romp in the tall, green grass. And take off your shoes while you're at it.

I will return to Zion, and will dwell in the midst of Jerusalem . . . And the streets of the city shall be full of boys and girls playing in its streets. (Zechariah 8:3,5)

Let lightness and joy into our sometimes heavy lives, O Gracious Spirit.

When the acid of hate turns to water

Water dripping on a stone can wear it away. Love and constant caring can destroy hate. When Julie and Michael Weisser moved to Lincoln, Nebraska, they immediately became targets of an obsessive bigot named Larry Trapp, a Grand Dragon of the Ku Klux Klan. They received his irrational and intense hatred because they were Jewish.

Threats, insults, and intimidation were his weapons. After their initial fear and repulsion, both Julie and Michael decided to meet Larry's vituperation with prayer and kindness. This decision did not come easily, and only after much reflection and inspiration from the Bible.

Suddenly, and without expectation, Larry Trapp began to respond. He renounced his bigotry, the horrors of his actions, and converted to Judaism. Suffering from complications of diabetes, he ended his life living with the Weissers.

God gave them as gifts to each other, miracles of love and faith in human nature and in God.

Strike the rock, and water will come out of it, so that the people may drink. (Exodus 17:6)

Give me, O Lord, a heart full of understanding and kindness.

The wonders of nature

The beauties of nature alone are reason enough to preserve and protect the environment. But nature offers us more. Healing herbs. Medicines. Even pesticides.

Neemix is a pesticide made from the seeds of the neem tree. The tree's fruit, leaves, roots and bark also possess good qualities. Its name in Sanskrit, arishth, means "reliever of sickness." The tree has long been known to residents of India and Burma. Now it's becoming known in the West.

A garden columnist quoted a report about the neem tree as saying, "Even some of the most cautious researchers are saying that neem deserves to be called a wonder plant." It is not harmful to lady bugs, butterflies, bees — or people.

We have a responsibility to be good stewards of the Earth. Afterall, we never know what hidden treasures, like the neem tree, it still holds.

It is required of stewards that they be trustworthy. (1 Corinthians 4:2)

Help us to appreciate the wonders of Your creation, Father.

A courageous athlete

Runner Tony Volpentest set a world record in Atlanta in the summer of 1996. The 23-year-old sprinter ran the 100 meter race in 11.36 seconds.

You may be thinking right now, "Volpentest? I don't remember him at the summer Olympics. Michael Johnson, Gail Devers, Donovan Bailey, sure — but Volpentest?"

Tony Volpentest, who was born without hands or feet, set that world record at the Paralympics, the games for the handicapped. He took up track in high school hoping to make friends. He now wears prostheses that imitate the muscle action of real feet.

By the way, his record of 11.36 seconds is only about a second and a half behind Donovan Bailey's, the world's fastest man.

This young man was probably told many times that there would be things he could never do, because of his handicaps. But his courage and determination proved everyone wrong.

Can you do the same?

When you walk, your steps will not be hampered; and if you run, you will not stumble. (Proverbs 4:12)

Lord, strengthen our faith in You and in ourselves.

Remembering all our children

There is a beautiful poem called "Children's Prayer" by Ina J. Hughes. It lists all kinds of children who need prayers.

"We pray for children
    who sneak popsicles before supper
    who erase holes in math workbooks
    who can never find their shoes."

These are the youngsters we easily recognize. There are others:

    "whose monsters are real . . .
    whose nightmares come in the daytime . . .
We pray . . . for those we never give up on
    and for those who don't get a second
    chance."

Think of them all: children of war and of famine, refugee children who travel endless dusty roads forced from their homes because of adult conflicts they do not understand, children of poverty who stare empty-eyed out of windows.

They are all our children. They are us. Let us pray and work for them.

Let the children come to Me. (Mark 10:4)

Show us how to have mercy on all the children of the world, Beloved Lord.

Triumph of the spirit

The human spirit is indomitable.

Take Brian Dickinson, a journalist for the Providence Journal Bulletin. Years after being diagnosed with amyotrophic lateral sclerosis (ALS), better known as Lou Gehrig's disease, the veteran newspaperman continues to turn out his column — despite the fact that he can't type, operate a keyboard, or hold a pencil. ALS may have taken his body but it hasn't conquered his mind.

Dickinson, aided and supported by his wife Barbara and his three sons, reports from the besieged front that is his body. Using a toggle switch to move a cursor on a screen, his columns, one of which can take 15 hours to write, have earned him a national award for commentary, and he and his wife harbor hopes of winning a Pulitzer.

Mrs. Dickinson provides the key to her husband's spirit when she says, "We decided we were going to concentrate on the living part of this."

It's a useful thought for the next time we're feeling sorry for ourselves.

Be courageous and valiant. (2 Samuel 13:28)

Help me in coping with my afflictions, Father.

Lost images of youth

College yearbooks have fallen on hard times. All over America there seems to be a decline in interest. Soon, you won't be able to leisurely leaf through the "Oakleaf" or the "Etosian" in the comfort of your living room and relive the crazy days, the dances, the athletic contests, the honor events, the relative freedom of your youth.

There are some schools that still hold to the tradition through sheer tenacity or creative marketing, but, as the times change, so does the medium for memories. Magazines, CD-ROM, videos, community bulletin boards . . . all manner of material are now available.

There has also been a decline in extracurricular college activities. As older students attend classes now, campuses grow more diverse.

There is less a sense of belonging. Change is important, but difficult. It is never easy to decide when to hold on, when to let go.

The memory of the righteous is a blessing. (Proverbs 10:7)

Lord, do not let me forget to remember.

When your kids compete

God wrote the originals. Now it seems as though every time one turns around there's another list of commandments. Here's one for parents whose children compete in sports:

■ Be sure that your children know that win or lose, scared or heroic, you love and appreciate them and aren't disappointed in them.

■ Be honest about their athletic ability.

■ Do not coach while taking them to or from the rink, track, court, field or pool.

■ Teach children to enjoy competition for its own sake.

■ Do not try to relive your athletic accomplishments or create in your children the athletic career you wanted but didn't have.

■ Do not compare your children's skills with others.

■ Understand that courage is relative. It isn't the absence of fear, but doing something despite fear.

Discipline your children, and they will give you rest; they will give delight to your heart. (Proverbs 19:17)

Holy Spirit, inspire mothers and fathers.

Patience makes perfect

Mem Shannon had hoped for a musical career but at 22 his father died. Faced with household bills, including his brother's college education, he started driving a cab.

Mem Shannon never gave up his dream of becoming a blues musician though. His guitar always rode with him in his cab and he would compose his music while waiting for passengers. The world that unfolded in his back seat and on the streets he travelled became his source of musical inspiration. After all, the blues are about everyday life and who could better comment than the observer who watches through the rear view mirror?

In 1995, after 13 years of perseverance, Shannon finally cut his first CD and became a hit with the jazz and blues scene. He says of his long wait for success, "I had a lot of patience when I was younger. Later on, I sometimes had to pray for it.

Mem Shannon knew that patience and success go hand in hand. Practice patience in your own life and remember that the only guaranteed failure is quitting.

We hope for what we do not see, we wait for it with patience. (Romans 8:25)

Abba, remind me that patience must be learned each and every day.

Deer pays unexpected visit to school

"Be prepared" is a pretty useful motto to live by. However, "expect the unexpected" might be a better one for the residents of Chisholm, Minnesota.

On an otherwise ordinary afternoon, a lost and frightened deer went tearing through Chisholm Middle School starting in the teachers' lounge. An amazed observer said, "It just jumped right through the window."

From the lounge, the animal ran down a hallway and into the weight room. "We were really surprised," said one of those working out when the deer showed up.

Eventually, things got back to normal. But heads were still shaking. "I really couldn't believe what I was seeing," said a school employee. "It was just unreal."

Preparation is a key to success. So is flexibility since we can't plan for every contingency.

Keep awake — for you do not know when the master of the house will come. (Mark 13:35)

Lord, help us rise to the occasion and face whatever challenges life brings.

Foul, not fair, coaches

Nine-year-old Nicholas Clark of Crown Point, Indiana, shocked everyone when he returned a trophy he had won as a member of the state champion Little League team. "The coaches treated me like scum," he told the president of the Little League board. "I don't want this."

Nicholas joined the baseball team to have fun. But it wasn't fun at all. He rarely got to play, and when he did, the other kids would call him names. His coaches did nothing to stop the taunts and berated him for not caring about winning.

Statistics show that 75% of kids drop out of their favorite sports. A major reason kids give is verbally abusive coaches who take the fun out of the game.

"Coaches have the opportunity to shape young men and women to be better people on and off the field," says Jim Deidinger of Derby, Kansas, who has won awards for his work coaching underprivileged youth.

You can be a "coach" to young people by helping, teaching and encouraging them.

While physical training is of some value, godliness is valuable in every way, holding promise for both the present life and the life to come. (1 Timothy 4:7-8)

Creator, guide us in letting boys and girls know how much value they have.

Breads for every life

Bread. Nowadays that rectangular, half plastic, bagged, squishy white basic for sandwiches and French toast and — if you're thrifty when it's gone stale — bread pudding.

Bread. Staff of life since humans first cultivated wild grains, ground them into flour and produced loaves, round or long, flat or thick.

Matzos, baguettes, and pitas. Braided challah, chapatti, and bagels. Tortillas, rough ryes and pumpernickels.

Health and sweet breads with fruit, nuts, seeds; or herbs, oils, olives, meat, cheese or chocolate.

Bread. Flour. Liquid. Usually but not always leavening and salt. Special shapes and ordinary.

Breads for every day. For celebrations. For worship. And called the staff of life by cultures around the world.

What sustains our life at every level, body, mind, heart and soul, does not have to be fancy, expensive or rare.

The ordinary, simple, honest, wholesome — and toothsome suffices.

Father, hallowed be Your name. Your kingdom come. Give us each day our daily bread. (Luke 11:2-3)

Feed us, Nurturing Father, with food for soul, mind and body.

Blow out your candles, Laura

It seems as if all major poets have had their muse. The muse for one of America's greatest playwrights was a diminutive woman named Rose. She was his older sister, and they were the only two Williams children.

Rose will always be known as the inspiration for Laura in "The Glass Menagerie." Tennessee wrote of Rose that she was his bulwark against his "haunted household."

In 1943, in an attempt to cure a mental problem, she was lobotomized, that is, part of her brain was destroyed. Her gentle spirit haunts "A Streetcar Named Desire" (Blanche), "The Night of the Iguana" (Hannah), and "Summer and Smoke" (Alma).

Rose died at age 87. Two years before, when she had blown out the candles on her birthday cake, Rose said she wished for "Life." As long as there is theater, Rose will live.

What part of yourself will you leave behind? What good will live after you?

Do not walk in the way of evildoers . . . for they cannot sleep unless they have done wrong. (Proverbs 4:14,16)

Protect those with mental illness, O Lord.

Helping others, creatively

Competitions of many kinds are used to raise money for charitable causes. Musicians and mimes, acrobats and actors compete in talent shows. But writers don't usually step into the spotlight.

In New York City last year, though, teams of poets from Brooklyn and Manhattan met in a competition. Judges used Olympic-type scoring to select winners, and the audience cheered contestants — or booed them.

Tickets to the match cost $6. Proceeds went to the city's largest soup kitchen. Its programs provide food, employment counseling, clothing, and medical care to over 300,000 people a year.

A rousing poetry competition is just one example of creative ways to help others.

Kindred and helpers are for a time of trouble. (Sirach 40:24)

Inspire our efforts to assist the needy, Holy Spirit.

Ordinary man and statesman

In some ways, he seems ordinary. Farmer. Teacher. Husband of 43 years. Grandfather. These days he enjoys gardening and attends daily Mass.

But Julius K. Nyerere is a leader whose name is indelibly written into the history of modern-day Africa. He is still sought out for advice and wisdom by political officials worldwide.

In 1962, Mr. Nyerere was elected the first President of Tanzania. At the time his country won independence from Britain in 1961, it was a collection of disparate tribes. He built it into a nation which experienced peace for decades. In 1985 he left office, handing over power to a constitutionally chosen successor.

Mr. Nyerere admits mistakes in his economic and political policies. Nevertheless, he left his country much improved in health and education.

Standing in his garden, he says, "It's very relaxing for people like myself who deal with politics, ideas . . . it's a great help if you can dirty your hands in some soil."

Happy is the person who meditates on wisdom . . . pursuing her like a hunter. (Sirach 14:20,22)

Holy Spirit, teach me the way to wisdom and simplicity.

Thank you, Ben

He invented the Franklin stove. He is credited with discovering electricity. He helped formulate the Declaration of Independence, and he was one of the most beloved and cherished of our Founding Fathers. His unique knack for invention, diplomacy and turn of phrase certainly insured his place in history. What you may not know was that Benjamin Franklin was instrumental in the development of the post office in the U.S.

In 1737 he was appointed Deputy Postmaster of Philadelphia, and in 1753 he became joint Postmaster General for the Northern British colonies. He was responsible for vast improvements to the Postal Service, including overnight delivery between Philadelphia and New York.

With the start of the Revolution, he was appointed head of the U.S. postal system under the Continental Congress. Two centuries later, Franklin is credited with laying the basis for the U.S. postal system.

It's good to know the origins of so much we take for granted.

No one after lighting a lamp puts it under the bushel basket, but on the lampstand, and it gives light to all in the house. (Matthew 5:15)

Grant that I may use my talents for Your honor and glory, Giver of every good gift.

The life of one man: God & music

"God's genius musician." That is what Austrians call composer Anton Bruckner.

It's impossible to talk about Bruckner without looking at the essential role St. Florian's Monastery played in his life.

When he was four, Bruckner's father, a schoolteacher, recognized his musical ability and gave him a small violin. Later he sent him to St. Florian's, where he distinguished himself playing the organ. Years later, when the organist position at the monastery became vacant, Bruckner was the logical successor. There, he managed to write 50 major and minor compositions.

Yet for all his growing fame, Bruckner would not let go of St. Florian's. Often he would return for rest and for solace. His greatest wish, to be buried at St. Florian's, was granted in 1896 when, to the sound of his own Mass in F minor, Bruckner was laid to rest in a simple sarcophagus beneath the huge organ he so loved.

A lesson to contemplate: life centered on the beauty of music and of God.

Praise the Lord with the lyre; make melody to Him with the harp of ten strings. (Psalm 33:2)

Let me always praise You, Lord, with all that You have given me.

The times they are a changin'

It comes as no surprise that the family has undergone some drastic and often unsettling changes in recent years. The traditional family, where mom stayed at home and father brought home the bacon, has become somewhat of an anomaly in an economy driven society. Today a two family income is almost a necessity for many.

Then, too, there has been a dramatic rise in "single parent families." Latch-key-children have become commonplace. In an effort to remedy this, the National Day of the Working Parent was inaugurated for September 9th.

Simultaneous rallies were held in Washington, New York and Chicago. Information boxes filled with child and elder-care materials were given to business people and politicians. More than 40 major public-TV stations offered a documentary series, "Families in the '90s."

We must learn to combine old-fashioned concern with new approaches to improve and preserve the family.

The man named his wife Eve, because she was the mother of all living. (Genesis 3:20)

Holy Spirit, inspire parents and children, grandparents, aunts and uncles to work together to improve and strengthen the family.

A parent's high purpose

The special responsibility of parents is to tap a child's unique strengths. Increasingly, experts in child development maintain that intelligence takes many forms. Daniel Goleman, author of *Emotional Intelligence,* includes creative powers and the ability to understand oneself and others as expressions of intelligence. And Dr. Howard Gardner makes the case for at least seven different intelligences, from musical and linguistic to bodily and interpersonal.

What can a parent do to encourage and develop children's learning power? Expose them early to music and art; live performances and concerts; dance exercises at home. Acquaint them with other languages at an early age. Buy children inexpensive cameras.

Emotional intelligence can affect success and well-being more then learning. Help your children find balance and contentment while developing their potential. God has given parents no higher purpose than this.

> **When He was twelve years old, they went up as usual. . . . After three days they found Him in the temple . . . Then He went down with them . . . and was obedient to them. (Luke 2:42,46,51)**

Teacher of us all, help me inspire my children.

Mothers team up for fun

What began as an impromptu basketball game between a group of mothers and their daughters, has taken off — and taken a new turn.

The 9- and 10-year-old girls play for a local park team in the Los Angeles area.

About forty of their moms formed the Moms Basketball League. They meet Sundays, break into teams and play — hard.

One of the player-moms, Sandy Banks, feels she has discovered a lot about competition and coping: "If you miss a couple of shots, you can't sit around feeling humiliated."

In spite of the aches and pains that come from "a tough game of basketball," the women enjoy themselves.

There's a special feeling that comes with exerting yourself. Putting yourself on the line can bring a sense of accomplishment. Whatever you want to accomplish, give it your best.

When a woman is in labor, she has pain . . . But when her child is born, she no longer remembers the anguish because of the joy of having brought a human being into the world. (John 16:21)

Spirit of Life, give me a zest for doing and being.

These earthen vessels

Few people would consider it a compliment to be called hard-hearted.

St. Irenaeus, the second century bishop of Lyons, France, and one of the first great Christian theologians, offered this reflection on the dangers of growing hard and harsh:

"It is not you who shapes God;
it is God who shapes you.
If then you are the handiwork of God,
await the hand of the Artist
who does all things in due season.
Offer the pottery of your heart, soft and tractable,
and keep well the form in which
the Artist has fashioned you.
Let your clay be moist,
lest you grow hard and lose
the imprint of the Potter's fingers."

Just like the clay in the potter's hand, so are you in My hand. (Jeremiah 18:6)

It is a tough world, I say to myself, Father. Show me how to risk myself by loving You and Yours above all.

A winner on and off the field

College athlete Jason Harty may seem like a tough guy when he's on the wrestling mat, but he's really got a tender heart.

The University of North Carolina student is not only a top student and athlete, he also devotes his free time to public service. He leads Carolina Outreach, an organization comprised of UNC student-athletes. Under his leadership, participation in the program has increased from eight teams doing seven projects to all 27 teams doing 25 projects. They give something back to the community, whether it's raising money for a good cause, running food and clothing drives or visiting kids at an orphanage.

Harty encourages his fellow participants to bring a light to others: "I tell the athletes, 'You don't know how blessed you are, and it doesn't take very much for you to give a little of yourself to people who would die to be where you are.'"

One young man is changing the world by helping those in his community.

Pursue what makes for peace and for mutual upbuilding. (Romans 14:19)

Lord, guide young people to service.

How much does it matter to you?

There are some things we say we want or believe we should want. But maybe not as much as we think we do.

There's a story about a young man in ancient time who wanted knowledge and understanding. He decided to ask the philosopher Socrates to help him.

Socrates agreed. He led his eager student to the seashore. They waded out and Socrates grabbed the young man, pushed his head under water and held him down while he struggled. Finally, Socrates released the sputtering youth.

"When you were under water, what was the one thing you wanted more than anything else?" asked Socrates.

The answer came without hesitation: "Air!"

Socrates said, "When you want knowledge and understanding as badly as you wanted air, you won't have to ask anyone to give it to you."

What's important to you? Is it as important as your next breath?

O Lord God . . . give me now wisdom and knowledge. (2 Chronicles 1:9,10)

Solomon asked You for wisdom, God. Guide me in desiring and seeking Your wisdom and Your will in all things, always.

A jungle queen

You wouldn't think that you could find a wild animal handler in the middle of the Bronx, New York.

But you can, and her name is Christina Regenhard. She has been working at Jungle World in the Bronx Zoo for the past three years, with an assortment of reptiles, fish and insects.

She wanted to work with animals all of her life: "I think I understood from an early age that animals tend to act the way they do for a reason. If you treat them with respect, they will treat you accordingly."

Up until about 10 years ago, the zoo staff was predominantly male. Now there are more women staffers than men. Christina waited for 9 years after putting in her initial application.

When you really want something, it's worth waiting for and working for.

Have dominion over the fish of the sea, the birds of the air, the cattle and all the animals that crawl on the earth. (Genesis 2:28)

Increase my reverence for Your creation, Lord.

Stay-at-home mom pops off

One mother passed up paid employment outside her home in order to be available to her young children and ended up creating a popular business which became a family project.

Robin Frederich of South Windsor, Connecticut, had vowed to be a stay-at-home mom. She and her husband Glen had decided this would be best for their children ages 8, 6 and 4. But when the bills came in they worried about a decision with such financial consequences.

Robin, who used to make caramel popcorn in her kitchen for family and friends, was pleased when her pastor praised it as "the best popcorn I've ever tasted." She hadn't thought of it as a business venture until her pastor displayed the snacks in *his* donut shop window. Robin's Gourmet Popcorn was born and became successful.

"One of the biggest blessings is being able to hire other moms who need extra income" and who want to be home for their young children, says Robin.

We ought to support such people. (3 John 8)

Give us the fortitude, God, to make wise decisions for our families.

Love letters

Linda Bremner, who lost her young son Andy to lymphoma, has found a way to honor his memory and in the process help thousands of children with similar terrible illnesses.

Knowing how Andy loved to greet the mailman and receive letters, Linda would send mail of her own creation to her son, signed "Your secret pal." Even though Andy eventually figured out that it was his mom authoring the secret pal letters, they meant the world to him.

Andy died in August of 1984, yet his mom is still writing those letters. Today, Linda Bremner is president of Love Letters, Inc., which weekly sends handmade cards and other items to some 1,000 seriously ill children. Working full-time for little pay, Bremner calls it a labor of love. As she says, "I will always write a love letter, and there will always be a child who needs one."

As a mother comforts her child, so I will comfort you. (Isaiah 66:13)

As you did, Lord Jesus, enable me to reach out with love.

Succeeding — in spite of the critics

The New York Times Book Review celebrated its 100th anniversary year not long ago. It's centennial issue included reprints of many classics that had been reviewed in its pages over the decades.

The *Book Review* also demonstrated a sense of humor, and probably chagrin, in mentioning some important volumes that it had panned.

H. G. Wells' *Invisible Man* has been a science fiction favorite for a century, but the original review said it overtaxed "the imagination of the reader." The heroine of L. M. Montgomery's *Anne of Green Gables* who has enchanted readers since 1908, didn't charm the reviewer. And the '50's *The Catcher in the Rye* by J. D. Salinger struck the critic as long, monotonous, and boring.

One said Joseph Heller's anti-war satire *Catch-22* "fails here because half its incidents are farcical and fantastic." Readers thought that was part of the novel's great attraction.

So, while criticism has its place, decide for yourself the quality of your efforts. If it is good, you will be the one with the last word.

Human success is in the hand of the Lord. (Sirach 10:5)

Don't let me dwell on others' criticism, Holy Spirit. And help me avoid being negative about others.

The healing power of art

Art not only heals, it can be a revelation from God. So discovered clinical counselor and writer Judi Bailey, who found art therapy to be just the balm for middle-age blues.

Through prayer and God's help, she got the message: take better care of the frightened child within the 43-year-old woman. A form of visual art enabled her to get in touch with a part of herself she had walled off.

Art can be a key to understanding and caring for the soul. Poetry, music, painting — all are expressions of prayer and homage to God. Artistic endeavors give us something substantial to do. At least for that time we can give up our worries and goals and attend to our spirits and God's world.

Seek to express insight and beauty. Know your Creator by getting in touch with creation.

> **If through delight in the beauty of (creation) people assumed them to be gods, let them know . . . the author of beauty created them . . . From the greatness and beauty of created things comes a corresponding perception of their Creator. (Wisdom of Solomon 13:3,5)**

> *Let me look, listen, and experience You in Your creation, Author of Beauty, Creation's Lord.*

The secrets of success

Who says money can't buy everything?

In Britain, some enterprising entrepreneurs want to help those people who don't think it's enough to have the right car, the right clothes, the right education, etc. These businessmen have all the right "extras" available.

For sale: fake ancestral portraits for your manor, libraries at $16 per inch of books, even glamorous "friends" you can rent for your next dinner party.

It's not enough to look successful. To truly be successful, we must contribute in some way to the good of others. Helping others is the most valuable thing we can give ourselves, others and our community.

You will not only earn the respect of others. You will earn respect for yourself. That's something no one else can sell you.

Serve one another with whatever gifts each of you has received. (1 Peter 4:10)

Jesus, show us how to achieve what's really important.

The message of belief

God knows, the world we inhabit is a vast, crowded and complex place. How does each of us make our way? All too often, out of fear and insecurity, we treat others with suspicion and disrespect. The history of humankind is marred with hundreds of wars, the result of an "us against them" mentality that has afflicted us from the days of Genesis.

The Torah states, "You shall love your neighbor as yourself, for I am God." Literally, this means that each of us must love the other because she or he is like me, and God gives each of us uniqueness. But once you reject the one God, hating your neighbor means that you each have your own god. Result? Strife, discord and destruction.

The true message of the belief in one God is that all humans are siblings. Today, try to look at that stranger down the street as a brother or sister.

Love one another with mutual affection; outdo one another in showing honor ... Contribute to the needs of the saints; extend hospitality to strangers ... Live in harmony with one another. (Romans 12:10,13,16)

Thank You for my family of fellow seekers, Creator.

The wonderful potential of children

Every child has creative potential. Whether it ever gets tapped can depend on the response of parents and other adults.

Experts suggest at least three ways to help youngsters recognize their latent abilities: encourage persistence; give positive feedback; support optimism.

"A lot of children are not persistent because they worry that a failure will mean they're not smart," says psychology professor Carol Dweck. "If we want children to be persistent, we must emphasize effort." Teach children how their hard work pays off and provide examples from your own experience.

Promote optimism by helping children view setbacks as temporary. Remind them of their past successes.

Positive feedback isn't the same as constant praise. It's preferable to support the child's interest in learning for its own sake. Explore their ideas. Ask how they figure out tough problems.

Children have potential. With guidance, they'll realize it.

Teach the way of God. (Mark 12:14)

Help us, Divine Teacher, to guide the children in our care.

Finding the right fit

One day, an older woman overheard a conversation between a mother and her son.

As the pair shared a bench with the woman, she heard the mother say, looking down at her child's feet: "Ryan, you have your shoes on the wrong feet."

"But," the little boy replied, taking a long, hard look at his feet and then up at his mother, "these are the only feet I got!"

The exchange between parent and child holds a lesson for all of us. God has made each of us with certain special gifts and talents which are only ours. And God has given us certain limitations as well. Each day of our lives is a challenge to find the right fit — just like a little boy found his challenge in making sure his shoes found the right feet!

Each day we are called, while working within our limitations, to use the gifts and talents God gave us to make the world a better place — to make a difference!

A man, going on a journey, summoned his slaves and entrusted his property to them; to one he gave five talents, to another two, to another one, to each according to his ability. (Matthew 25:14-15)

Father, help me know and do Your will today.

It's all about a four-letter word

A college professor once had his sociology class go into the Baltimore slums to get case histories of 200 young boys. They were asked to write an evaluation of each boy's future. Their unanimous decision: they haven't got a chance.

Some 25 years later, another sociology professor, reading the earlier study, decided to do some follow-up. With the exception of 20 boys who had died or moved away, the remaining students from the slums had all achieved more than ordinary success as lawyers, doctors and businessmen.

The professor pursued the matter further, asking each one the reason for his success. From each, the reply came: "There was a teacher . . ."

The professor found that teacher, quite old, yet still very alert. What was her "magic formula"? "It's really very simple," she said. "I loved those boys."

Love builds up. (1 Corinthians 8:1)

Send Your Spirit, Lord, to help me love as You love.

Courage, the toughest virtue

What is courage?

Webster defines it as "mental or moral strength to . . . withstand danger, fear, or difficulty."

That is one definition.

But are there non-dictionary definitions of courage?

How about these courage-in-action definitions for starters?

- asking unpopular questions
- listening to difficult answers
- carrying on when weary
- resisting peer pressure
- refusing to use violence
- giving up unrealistic expectations

There are, if you watch closely, many obscure definitions of courage-in-action. The college student away from home for the first time. The young single finding that first apartment and first job. The new parent. The chronically ill child or adult. The new widow or widower. The isolated elderly pensioner.

Love may make the world go 'round. But courage makes love possible.

Take courage; I have conquered. (John 16:33)

Jesus, share Your courage with us.

Keeping a dream alive

In Beacon, New York, a small Hudson River city, a man named Charles Dent read a story.

It was a historical tale, in fact, about Italy's Leonardo da Vinci and the 24-foot bronze charger that the artist conceived, but never completed.

"Let's give Leonardo his horse!" Dent said after reading the magazine article about da Vinci's seemingly lost dream. And, for the next 17 years, Dent dedicated his life to building the horse, traversing the globe to talk to da Vinci scholars, culling old sketches of the horse, and setting up a nonprofit organization that would fund the $3.2 million project.

Then Dent died.

But his dream — da Vinci's dream, that is — did not die with him. In fact, the organization Dent set up is still funding the project's completion, now set for the end of this century.

With a little dedication and a lot of work, dreams can come true.

Let the favor of the Lord our God be upon us, and prosper for us the work of our hands. (Psalm 90:17)

You, Master, are Lord of all. Give Your blessing to the work of our hands — and our minds.

A kick and a hug

Greatly shaken by her parents' bitter separation and the death of a beloved aunt, Jill Davis was a true discipline problem for the Sisters who taught her in the first through third grades.

"I had to stay after school hundreds of times," Davis said, as punishment for her many disruptive emotional outbursts.

Then came the fourth grade — and Sister Lucia.

In fact, Sister Lucia seemed amused during one of Davis' angry demonstrations. This infuriated the young girl, who tried to kick the good teacher. "Thank heaven," Davis recalled, "I only harmlessly rustled her skirts."

After the action, Davis froze, waiting for the Sister's next move. Sister Lucia bent down and embraced her, hugging her tightly for a long time.

"I felt myself melting," Davis remembered. "Try as I might, I could not choke back the sobs. My tears carried away some of the pain I'd been suppressing for so long, and I felt calm again."

Often, anger's best match is loving kindness.

(God) . . . does not retain His anger forever, because He delights in showing clemency. (Micah 7:18)

Break through my anger Lord; bring me Your peace.

Caring for those in need

For over half-a-century, CARE has provided the link between American donors of food, books and tools and victims around the world whose lives have been ripped apart by wars.

Now the organization is focusing on domestic victims as well. Recognizing the urgent need to help American children develop better reading skills, CARE started a pilot program in Boston. It encourages parents to get into the habit of reading with their children at home.

CARE delivers packages of books, cassettes and instructions to parents of thousands of pupils in the city's public schools. The organization's efforts at promoting literacy and learning are timely and appreciated.

As 5-year-old Akim Williams said upon receiving his CARE package at a local social center, "Reading makes you really smart."

Keep reading and encouraging others.

Help the poor for the commandment's sake, and in their need do not send them away empty-handed. (Sirach 29:9)

Let my mind be eager and open to learning, Lord.

"Thank you" — for a gift well used

Middlebury, Vermont, held an informal community appreciation day for Dr. Wayne Peters.

Trained as a pediatrician, he opened his practice in Middlebury in 1965. But since then he has delivered babies, cared for adults and taught classes at Middlebury's hospital and schools in addition to being a pediatrician.

And it hasn't been for the money. Says Dr. Brakeley, his associate, "He's bartered services . . . (seen) kids anywhere . . . to save their parents the cost of . . . the emergency room." Actually, he's refused no one for lack of payment.

He also hired Middlebury's first woman physician, Dr. Jody Brakeley, to be a part of his practice.

The grace to practice a trade, profession or skill is given for the good of all. The challenge is to use well the gifts you've been given.

Each of us was given grace according to the measure of Christ's gift . . . to equip the saints for the work of ministry, for building up the body of Christ. (Ephesians 4:7,12)

Enable us to use well all the gifts You've given us, Lord.

If not higher

A Jewish tale speaks of a rabbi in a Russian village who vanished every Friday for several hours. The villagers boasted that during that time their rabbi ascended to heaven to talk with God.

One Friday morning, a skeptical newcomer decided to find out the truth about the Friday trip. He hid near the rabbi's house, watched him rise and say his prayers. The rabbi then went into the forest. He chopped down a tree, and gathered a large bundle of wood, which he took to a shack in the poorest section of the village. He left the wood — enough for one week — with the old woman in that shack. The rabbi then quietly returned home.

The newcomer stayed in the village and became a disciple of the rabbi. And whenever he hears one of his fellow villagers say, "On Friday morning our rabbi ascends all the way to heaven," the newcomer quietly adds, "If not higher."

Sometimes others teach us without ever saying a word.

Lay up your treasure according to the commandments of the Most High . . . alms-giving . . . will rescue you from every disaster. (Sirach 29:11,12)

King of the Ages, may others come to know You through our charitable deeds.

Pray, at all times, everywhere

Father James Keller, the founder of The Christophers, penned some thoughts on St. Paul's famous advice to "pray always" as well as on prayer itself.

Father Keller wrote, "Paul was a realist who knew that ordinary people had neither the time nor inclination to devote long periods to contemplation . . . But if you are to be followers of Christ . . . you must be men and women of prayer."

Then he goes on to say that we can find occasions for prayer "in the eyes of a child . . . waiting for a stop light . . . putting a letter in the mail box . . . in a lover's embrace or after a stinging conflict . . . on a crowded street or utterly alone . . . in the kitchen, office or assembly line."

A quarter-century later we can add newer occasions for prayer, such as keying into a computer . . . the e-mail . . . pumping iron . . . chauffering the kids . . . waiting in line at the supermarket . . .

Wherever you are, there are occasions for prayer.

Pray without ceasing. (1 Thessalonians 5:17)

Master, show me how to pray.

Preserving diversity, preventing famine

Civil war decimated Rwanda beginning in 1994. Refugees fled westward into Zaire — itself convulsed by civil unrest.

One casualty: loss of genetic diversity in the basic food crops of beans, grains and starchy tubers. This genetic diversity, the result of both natural selection and careful farming, had insured bountiful harvests in each micro-climate with its unique soils, pests and parasites.

During the civil war almost half of all Rwandans were killed or displaced. Weeds, pests and plant diseases took over abandoned farms. When they could return, famine forced the people to eat what seeds they found.

The International Center for Tropical Agriculture began "Seeds of Hope." Seeds for the most important food crops were rescued, multiplied, and distributed to farmers.

Preserving the genetic diversity of food crops unique to a country is a long-term way to prevent famine and preserve human dignity.

I would feed you with the finest of the wheat, and with honey from the rock I would satisfy you. (Psalm 81:16)

Inspire agronomists and farmers as they work to supply food while preserving the genetic diversity of food crops, Lord of the harvest.

A man of his word

Danny O'Neil helped lead his college football team to one of the most important tournaments, the Rose Bowl.

As a result, a pro football team called him to try out for a place on their team. He turned them down for something more important.

The Kansas City Chiefs called and told him he needed to get on the next plane immediately to try out. O'Neil told them he had a Bible study with his high school students that night — could he catch a plane tomorrow?

The team told him no — he had to either come that day or forget about it. O'Neil realized he had a choice: keep his commitment to the kids or go for the NFL. He had told the teens he would be there for them, and he kept his word.

O'Neil chose to stay with his Bible study group, and now plays with an arena football team in Anaheim, California. It's not the NFL, but he is helping some of today's youth "tackle" the problems that face them today.

It takes a strong person to stand up to the courage of a conviction.

I regard everything as loss because of the surpassing value of knowing Christ Jesus my Lord. (Philippians 3:8)

May we learn to put things in perspective, Gracious Lord.

A song of peace

In the last years of his short life the Deacon Francis of Assisi composed his "Canticle of the Creatures." And at one desperate moment he had two of his friars sing it in Assisi's town square.

It seems that the Mayor and the Bishop of Assisi got into a terrible argument. The Bishop excommunicated the Mayor. The Mayor called up his private army. The Bishop called up his. Out of pride the two sides refused to listen or to talk with each other. Civil war loomed.

St. Francis' friars sang, in part, "Praise be to Thee my Lord for those / who pardon grant for love of Thee / And bear infirmity and tribulation, / Blessed be those who live in peace, / For by Thee Most High they shall be crowned."

The Mayor and the Bishop listened. Tears flowed. They embraced. The Bishop lifted the excommunication. The Mayor forgave the Bishop. They each sent their armies home.

Words can avert wars, reconcile enemies, bring peace. Or do the opposite. Respect the power of words. Use them for good, for peace.

Look! On the mountain the feet of one who brings good tidings, who proclaims peace! (Nahum 1:15)

Open our mouths in words of peace, Holy Spirit.

Walking on water

Basilisk. According to Webster's Dictionary, they're related to Iguanas. And noted for being able to run on their rear legs.

One of these tiny lizards is known as the Jesus Christ lizard. You see, it walks on water. Naturally. Literally.

Harvard University researchers James Glasheen and Thomas McMahon studied this basilisk with a high-speed video camera.

It seems that the basilisk's hind foot slaps the surface of pond or brook fast enough to create an air-filled hole. Before that can collapse, it pulls its feet out of the hole. And creates new ones. Hence the Jesus Christ lizard's ability to walk on water.

Walking on water is the basilisk's way to adapt and get around.

You have your God-given intelligence. Use it and prayer to enhance the quality of your life, to adapt and get around.

The days of our life are seventy years, or perhaps eighty, if we are strong. (Psalm 90:10)

Lord, You brought Your disciples' boat to safe harbor, walking on water to calm a storm. Bring my boat to safe harbor after a wise and prayer-filled life.

More than a motto

Next time you empty your pocket or purse of loose change, give it a second look. Besides portraits of presidents, pictures of eagles or buildings or other symbols, there are words. Among them is the phrase: *In God We Trust*. Wonder how that got there?

Thank the Rev. Mr. M. R. Watkinson of Ridleyville, Pennsylvania. He was a pastor there during the Civil War. In 1861 he wrote to Salmon P. Chase, Secretary of the Treasury. He said, "One fact touching our currency has hitherto been seriously overlooked. I mean the recognition of the Almighty God in some form on our coins."

He proposed a motto on the theme of God, Liberty and Law. Chase saw merit in the idea and instructed the director of the Philadelphia Mint to have a device prepared that would recognize "the trust of our people in God."

In 1864 the words In God We Trust appeared on a two-cent piece. They have been used ever since.

As individuals as well as a nation, let's remember to trust in God.

Those who trust in the Lord are like Mount Zion. (Psalm 125:1)

You deserve my faith and trust, Holy Lord. Strengthen my belief in Your loving Providence.

Love-ly thoughts

Is there any subject more dreamed about, sung about or written about than love? And it isn't only in spring when romance is in the air. Human beings can be enraptured 365 days a year.

While like all good things love can be abused, it can also be life-giving. Here are a few thoughts on the much pondered subject of romantic love from *Bits & Pieces* magazine:

Love is an unusual game. There are either two winners or none.

Love doesn't make the world go 'round, it makes the ride worthwhile.

Love is what makes two people sit in the middle of a bench when there's plenty of room at both ends.

The most important thing a father can do for his children is to love their mother.

And a final word from poet Robert Frost: "Love is an irresistable desire to be irresistibly desired."

Set me as a seal upon your heart, as a seal upon your arm; for love is strong as death, passion fierce as the grave . . . Many waters cannot quench love, neither can floods drown it. (Song of Solomon 8:6,7)

Grant grace to lovers, Dear Lord and Lover.

A kind heart — and duct tape

Writer Michael Warren tells of this frightening experience when he was a teenager. He and his family were driving through the desert to Arizona when their radiator blew — leaving them stranded.

They prayed for help — and got it. A beat-up old car came along and a shabbily dressed man got out. He patched up their radiator with duct tape. Then he accompanied them to Tucson, in case they had any more trouble.

They drove close behind their rescuer, thinking about the message on his bumper sticker. It read, "Lord, make me an instrument of your peace."

Remembering the incident, Warren says, "Sharing the peace of God . . . doesn't require heroics or special education. Sometimes a kind heart and a length of duct tape will do just fine."

How beautiful upon the mountains are the feet of the messenger who announces peace. (Isaiah 52:7)

Open my mind and heart to opportunities to make peace, to be at peace, to share peace with others, God.

Nun brings cheer and gets some in return

It's understandable when a person who is sick withdraws a little to take care of their own needs. It's inspirational when they're able to reach out and help others despite their difficulties.

Sister Eileen Horan of the Sisters of St. Joseph, a former teacher and principal, found a ministry boosting the spirits of shut-ins by sending cards and letters with inspirational messages, poems or prayers.

When she became a shut-in herself, Sister Horan, a big basketball fan, found herself on the receiving end of good cheer from a particularly treasured source. Jim Calhoun, the men's basketball coach at the University of Connecticut, sent her a letter along with a T-shirt, autographed team photo and a UConn basketball book. "When I wrote back to (the coach), I told him, 'They play and we pray.'"

One recipient of Sister Horan's notes thanked her for lifting his spirits and wrote they "seem to arrive when they are most needed."

Pray for one another, so that you may be healed. (James 5:16)

Give me the grace, Lord, to think of others whose needs may be greater than my own.

Reluctant but deserving heroes

Magda Trocme is a heroine in the eyes of many for her role in helping to rescue thousands of French Jews and others from the Nazis during World War Two.

Apparently Mrs. Trocme, who died in 1996 at age 94, didn't consider her actions all that remarkable. But along with her husband André, the charismatic pastor of the French Reformed Church in Chambon, she helped organize their entire village to hide and feed people who otherwise faced certain death.

One of those who survived thanks to the villagers of Chambon was Pierre Sauvage, a documentary film producer. He told the story in "Weapons of the Spirit." It was also told by Philip Hallie in his award-winning book, "Lest Innocent Blood Be Shed."

The Trocmes and their neighbors refused to be complacent. Or to ignore the "Golden Rule." They took risks in dangerous times. Truly they were heroic.

Do not repay anyone evil for evil . . . so far as it depends on you, live peaceably with all. . . . Do not be overcome by evil, but overcome evil with good. (Romans 12:17,18,21)

Inspire me, Holy Spirit, to act with courage.

Tree musketeers

A troop of 8-year-old Brownies used paper plates on a camping trip. And planted a tree to help replace the ones used for the paper plates. That was the beginning of a young people's organization called "Tree Musketeers."

The group initiated a tree-planting project to reduce air pollution in their town by planting over 700 trees. They also opened a recycling center. And publish an environmental magazine read by 50,000 young people.

The "Tree Musketeers," run by young people, has inspired others around the country.

To young people who often feel powerless, one of the "Tree Musketeers'" founders says, "Don't ever let anyone tell you that you can't change the world."

> **God said, "Let the earth put forth . . . fruit trees of every kind . . ." And it was so. The earth brought forth . . . trees of every kind. . . . And God saw that it was good. (Genesis 1:11-12)**

> *Creator, remind young people that they can change the world, starting with themselves.*

Footprints of God

A traveler sat outside his tent in the Sahara Desert talking with a young Bedouin guide about the meaning of life. The guide was convinced that the universe was designed and ruled by an all-wise Being. The traveler objected. "Nobody can know for certain that there is a God."

The young man pointed to a stretch of sand with a track of footprints: "When I see those footprints in the sand, I know that some person passed this way. Only a human being could have made them."

Then he pointed to the fading colors of the sunset and first stars appearing in the evening sky. "When I see the sun, and the moon, and the starry heavens in their beauty, I know that the Creator has passed this way. They are the footprints of God," said the guide.

Some argue that there is no proof of God's existence. But faith can only be satisfied by the knowledge and wisdom of souls touched by God. Don't worry. God can handle normal human doubts.

The Lord answered Job . . . "Can you bind the chains of the Pleiades, or loose the cords of Orion? (Job 38:1,31)

Teach me, Holy Spirit, not to fear moments of doubt, but to entrust them to You.

A third degree — before nine holes

The story is told about a "dignified and wealthy" British lawyer who desperately wanted to play the exclusive Sandringham golf course. Told that a member would have to vouch for him, he found a familiar figure who happened to be a member.

And thus a third degree began. The member wanted to know his religion and his wife's. And, oh, yes, his education; what sports he played; and whether he had served in the military. And if he'd seen military service, why then at what rank and in what campaigns? Finally, which languages did he speak?

The lawyer answered all these questions truthfully. And waited with baited breath for the member's decision: "nine holes."

If a half game of golf was that important to a "dignified and wealthy" British lawyer . . . What's equally and uniquely important to you? Having priorities simplifies life.

(Wisdom) cannot be gotten for gold, and silver cannot be weighed out as its price. (Job 28:15)

Holy Spirit, help me get my priorities straight.

Kosher in Utah

Ranchers in the economically struggling San Luis Valley of Colorado wanted to treat Israel's Minister of Agriculture to kosher buffalo meat.

They enlisted a rabbi's help. And after the Agriculture Minister had left they realized they'd become "experts."

That led to a kosher-meat cooperative that's the last word in ecumenism not to mention profitability. Mormon farmers. Hispanic Catholic cowboys. An east coast rabbi who explained koshering in a Knights of Columbus hall.

About 100 head of cattle and more than that of lambs are processed each week to supply kosher meat to Western cities. And, the ranchers and farmers aren't economically hard-pressed anymore.

There's a well-worn saying that one good turn deserves another. Here's another example of its truthfulness.

> **Abraham . . . said (to Sarah), ". . . three measures of choice flour, knead it, and make cakes." Abraham . . . took a calf . . . and gave it to the servant, who hastened to prepare it. Then he took curds and milk and the calf . . . and set it before them. (Genesis 18:6-8)**

> *Lord, You spread a banquet of manna and quail and water-from-the-rock. Reward those who have extended hospitality to me.*

What you are, what you owe

Albert Schweitzer was a man of many talents. A gifted musician, theologian and writer, he left an academic career to become a medical missionary in Africa. In 1952 he won the Nobel Peace Prize for his humanitarian work.

But he never forgot what he owed to others. He said: "I look back upon my youth and realize how many people gave me help, understanding, courage — very important things to me — and they never knew it. They entered into my life and became powers within me.

"All of us live spiritually by what others have given us, often unwittingly, in the significant hours of our life. At the time these significant hours may not even be perceived. We may not recognize them until years later when we look back, as one remembers some long-ago music or a boyhood landscape.

"We all owe to others much of gentleness and wisdom that we have made our own; and we may well ask ourselves what will others owe to us."

Owe no one anything, except to love one another; for the one who loves another has fulfilled the law. (Romans 13:8)

Help me give my best to others, Divine Friend, as You give Yourself to us all.

More beatitudes

Beatitudes. They offer some food for thought. Here are some adaptations of Jesus' originals.

■ Blessed are those who can laugh at themselves . . .

■ Blessed are those who know a mountain from a molehill . . .

■ Blessed are those who can relax and not need to make excuses . . .

■ Blessed are those who don't take themselves too seriously . . .

■ Blessed are those who know when to be still and listen . . .

■ Blessed are those who appreciate a smile, forget a frown . . .

■ Blessed are those who think before acting, pray before thinking.

The goal of the original Beatitudes as well as these modern ones is to sharpen our ability to recognize God in every person we meet. That's more than enough reason to live them moment by moment.

My heart says, "seek His face!" Your face, Lord, do I seek. (Psalm 27:8)

Keep me steadfast in living out the beatitudes, Jesus.

What's lasting

A life-like 8,000-man terra-cotta army complete with war-horses is being excavated from Emperor Qin Shi Huang's 2,200-year-old tomb outside Xian, China.

It took over half a million laborers 36 years to build it. And rebels a short time to burn the mausoleum and Huang's palace and kill his family.

What is remembered about Qin Shi Huang's short reign are his efforts to unify the diverse peoples of China. He defeated six states and a feudal nobility to begin a dynastic system that lasted until this century.

He also used hundreds of thousands of forced laborers and huge tax levies to build the protective Great Wall.

He standardized China's weights and measures as well as its written language and currency.

And it is these that are truly memorable. More so, even, than Huang's tomb and terra-cotta army.

Life is short and uncertain. Physical monuments can be destroyed. Build a reputation for doing good.

The human body is a fleeting thing, but a . . . good name lasts forever. (Sirach 41:11,13)

Savior, encourage my efforts to build the lasting monument of a lifetime of good deeds.

The gift of you

Did you ever think of yourself as a gift? You are, you know.

Perhaps you're wrapped in exquisite gift-wrap, all beribboned and bowed.

Or your wrapping is plain, ordinary. No ribbons. No bows.

Perhaps you've been mishandled in the "mail." Damaged. Even if it's not obvious at first.

But that's not the gift which is you. That's just the outside.

But inside. Ah, there's the gift that is you.

You in all your uniqueness. Your special personality. Your intelligence. Your talents. Your vision. Your perception of the world. Your hopes, fears, dreams. And your faults.

Look inside yourself. Accept the gift of yourself that God has made to you. Share your gift with others as they share their gift with you.

Remember. "A friend is a gift not just for me but to others through me."

God gives wealth and possessions and whom He enables to enjoy them, and to accept their lot and find enjoyment in their toil — this is the gift of God. (Ecclesiastes 5:19)

Thank You for each and every gift, Generous Lord.

A mother's legacy

Benjamin Bolger seemed like a normal child, but he was not. He suffered from severe dyslexia, a baffling neurological disease that affects as many as 26 million Americans. It is an inability to decode written words.

Loretta Bolger took her son out of an unproductive and impossible learning situation and began his schooling at home. Armed with her master's degree in elementary education, she created a curriculum that did not rely on printed or written material. She read to her son constantly. As with most dyslexics, Ben has a sharp mind and a retentive memory. He was ready for college at 13. His mother went with him.

At 19, he is one of the youngest ever admitted to the Yale law school. Loretta Bolger still reads to him from the law tomes, even though she is severely disabled from a near fatal automobile accident suffered when Ben was 10.

Some people have much asked of them. And they give all they can.

Do not neglect to show hospitality to strangers, for by doing that some have entertained angels without knowing it. (Hebrews 13:2)

Speak Your words to me, O Lord.

Finding a solution

Ethical and moral dilemmas constantly confront us in ways we might not anticipate.

Take the issue of the sea lions that are drawn to the salmon runs in Seattle's inland waterways. Fishermen and city authorities turned to marine biologists for help in stopping the appealing, but predatory seal lions from devouring the salmon. Enter Fake Willy, a 16-foot faux whale. He lurks beneath the surface of Puget Sound to scare the sea lions away from their helpless prey.

All involved are hoping Fake Willy will help solve the problem. The alternative? Kill the sea lions before they kill the salmon. That is a solution no one seems eager to embrace. At least, Fake Willy has called attention to a complex issue.

With cooperation, good intentions, and continual effort, even the thorniest of dilemmas can be considered and conquered.

> **Not only the creation but we ourselves . . . groan inwardly while we wait for . . . redemption. (Romans 8:23)**

> *Holy Spirit, give me the will to think before I act.*

An ancient tale gets new life

Are ancient Greek epics too difficult and irrelevant for modern-day elementary school children? No. At least not when they have an enthusiastic adult as their guide to adventure.

In Norwich, Vermont, youngsters seem to delight in reading Homer's *Odyssey* and interpreting it for today. Their teacher David Millstone "is just so awesome," said one student. "He makes the *Odyssey* so much fun!"

The fifth graders hear the tale read by parents and teachers. Then they read various interpretations of the poem and argue about the messages it contains. Later in the year they pick episodes to present to first graders, who are not too young to appreciate a good story.

Mr. Millstone doesn't think the *Odyssey* is too hard for youngsters. "Action and adventure, romance and love, magic and monsters, courage and cowardice . . . It's a rare child who cannot get interested in at least part of this story."

Render service . . . as to the Lord and not to men and women, knowing that whatever good we do, we will receive the same again from the Lord. (Ephesians 6:7-8)

Enable us, Lord, to hear your message and share it with enthusiasm.

Dare mighty things

It's easy enough to criticize and find fault with the actions of others. It's far more difficult to get personally involved in the nitty gritty of life and risk criticism.

"The credit belongs to the person who is actually in the arena; whose face is marred by dust and sweat and blood; who strives valiantly; who errs and comes short again and again," wrote Theodore Roosevelt.

"Who does actually strive to do deeds; who knows the great enthusiasms, the great devotion, spends oneself in a worthy cause; who at the best knows in the end the triumph of high achievement; and who at worst, if he or she fails, at least fails while daring greatly.

"Far better it is to dare mighty things, to win glorious triumphs even though checkered by failure, than to rank with those timid spirits who neither enjoy nor suffer much because they live in the grey twilight that knows neither victory nor defeat."

Take courage, all you people ... says the Lord; work, for I am with you ... according to the promise that I made you when you came out of Egypt. My spirit abides among you; do not fear. (Haggai 2:4,5)

Give me the courage to overcome my fears and to take more risks in life, Dear Jesus.

Teamwork to restore old church

The Great Stone Church at Mission San Juan Capistrano is due for restoration. Funding will determine how much of the needed work will get done.

The Roman-style church was built in 1806. Apparently quite magnificent for its time, it was the largest stone church in the United States. "It's kind of an American Acropolis," according to Jerry Miller, mission administrator. "Pretty soon, it will be a pile of rubble. Unless we act now, there will be nothing left."

Preservationists from the University of Pennsylvania are among those working to repair this architectural wonder. They're joined by local architects, structural engineers and masons. Memorial tiles being sold for $100 to $300 and private donations help fund the project.

"It's a labor of love," said one project worker. "It's important to give people an understanding of what a place was like. It gives you a clue to the past."

The Lord is in His holy temple. (Habakkuk 2:20)

Lord, encourage our attempts to work together for the betterment of our communities.

Expect the unexpected

Mark Podwal has learned that life doesn't always turn out the way one expects.

As a young medical student, Podwal dabbled in art. Today the 51-year-old physician is more of an artist than ever and finds himself with two flourishing careers.

Dr. Podwal creates art works with distinctly religious themes. One commission was for a 9-foot-by-6-foot ark curtain and finely embroidered Torah covers for Temple Emanu-El in New York City.

"It was a challenge to make it traditional, yet contemporary — and have the temple approve it," said Dr. Podwal.

Having our lives develop in ways different from early expectations makes things interesting. But we shouldn't be surprised at this turn of events.

Dr. Podwel explains it with a Yiddish proverb: "If you want to give God a good laugh, tell him your plans."

The human mind plans the way, but the Lord directs the steps. (Proverbs 16:9)

God, remind me to keep You in mind as I make plans for my life.

Autumn leaves, autumn tales

October serves as a colorful and refreshing seasonal way-station between the extremes of summer past and winter to come.

Dazzling foliage abounds, flies and mosquitoes all but disappear, and there's a crisp bite in the air that cries out for sweaters and jackets. Yes, the days grow shorter. Yet we experience, in the words of writer Maxine Kumin, the "briefest and most beautiful moment of stasis . . . Every day is more precious than the preceding. Dusk comes earlier in sharper air. The horses' coats thicken, blurring their summer-sleek outlines. Everything proclaims: We are reluctant. We are ready."

That seems the story of our lives: reluctant *and* ready. Let us count our blessings today, knowing full well that dusk comes early.

For everything there is a season, and a time for every matter under heaven. (Ecclesiastes 3:1)

Thank You, God, for the natural beauty of the seasons.

A window on history

James H. Billington is a man on a mission. He's bringing the Library of Congress into the computer age.

Mr. Billington is America's Librarian of Congress. Under his leadership items from the library's vast collections are going on-line. This will make it possible for ordinary men, women and children to personally view fascinating documents from our nation's history even if they can't travel to Washington, D.C.

With access to the Internet — perhaps through the local library — a child might read the 1884 diary of the 25-year-old future president, Teddy Roosevelt. Or, the notebooks of poet Walt Whitman; pamphlets by Frederick Douglass; the papers of anthropologist Margaret Mead.

"The main thing is that everybody gets a look at the American past," said Billington. "It's like finding your grandparents' letters in the attic."

Being able to look closely at our past ought to help us better plan for the future.

Remember the days of old, consider the years long past. (Deuteronomy 32:7)

May I always appreciate the importance of those who came before me, Jesus.

A Zen master's lessons in living

Do you feel you must first become an expert or consult an expert before you can take some action?

In their book, *Instructions to the Cook: A Zen Master's Lessons in Living a Life that Matters,* Bernard Glassman and Rick Fields suggest a different approach. The Zen way isn't that of expert but of beginner.

"Babies don't read books about walking or go to walking seminars. They just stand up, take a step, and fall down. Then they do it all over again. They might get frustrated or angry when they fall, but they don't get discouraged. They don't say, 'See, that proves that I can't walk! I'll never learn to walk. Walking is impossible!'"

We also must keep at it and not avoid the things that frighten us. We'll never have all the answers. We'll just develop greater understanding, clarity and "ability to deal with things as they . . . keep arising, endlessly."

Life can teach us simple yet profound lessons if we are willing to learn.

Consider the lilies of the field, how they grow. (Matthew 6:28)

Thank You, Lord, for Your beloved little children. Help us learn from them.

Moderation is the key

Let's face it, we Americans are a paradoxical people.

Poll after poll indicates our desire to stay healthy and fit, yet most of us say we are overweight, aren't exercising enough, still smoke too much, and are stressed out. We try to do the right things but more often than not feel we're fighting a losing battle.

More than ever before, moderation and common sense might be the cornerstone of a healthier, happier lifestyle.

Cut back on coffee and alcohol. Walk as often as possible. Perhaps a yoga class and practicing meditation will alleviate some of that stress. You don't have to eat dessert every night, and try to eat your big meal earlier in the day.

Oh, and don't forget prayer. Talking to God can help your heart, soul and body immeasurably.

We have this treasure in clay jars, so that it may be made clear that this extraordinary power belongs to God and does not come from us. (2 Corinthians 4:7)

You gave us form, Lord; may we treat our bodies wisely.

Praise today for tomorrow

Were you ever praised too much as a child? Chances are just the opposite: you probably wished you had felt the glow of your parents' admiration and rarely did. Many moms and dads are so afraid of giving their youngsters big egos that they err on the negative side.

Certainly, parents have a responsibility to correct children. But "most parent/child relationships suffer from praise deficit," according to psychologist Eva Feindler. The result can be young people who grow into adults that lack confidence and are overly self-critical.

Rather than targeting grades or sports, let youngsters know you admire aspects of their character. If they are especially good at listening, being a friend, showing kindness or honesty, let them know it.

What would you have given when you were little to have the most important people in the world, your folks, praise you? If they did — great! If not, don't lose your opportunity to give others the praise they need and deserve. Including yourself.

Give yourself the esteem you deserve. (Sirach 10:28)

Thank You, Divine Friend, for every word of praise and encouragement You have spoken to me through another.

Inventing things that think

If you think the computer has taken over the world, just wait.

Forget about desktops and laptops, within the next few years you will able to wear a computer. The screen could be in your eyelgasses or on your wrist. And the microprocessor in your shoe will be recharged every time you take a walk.

The Media Lab at the Massachusetts Institute of Technology is attempting to add intelligence to ordinary objects through the Things That Think project.

Other possibilities are a refrigerator that alerts you when you are out of milk or when it turns sour, a doorknob that identifies the person opening it, or a desk that keeps track of where you file things.

Professor Neil Gershenfeld, the project's co-director says they "can do most of this in the laboratory now."

Whatever the future holds, we can't predict it. But we can prepare ourselves by being open to knowledge and, even more important, to wisdom.

Happy are those who find wisdom and . . . get understanding. (Proverbs 3:13)

The world gets no easier to live in, God, but it is still Yours.

An extra special treat

One Halloween evening, Deacon Tom Lewis was trying to prepare a homily with a short, inspiring example of the spirit of sharing. All his ideas that night just didn't seem to work. Adding to his frustration was the constant interruption by neighborhood young people who were playing "Trick or Treat."

As the evening went on, Deacon Lewis eventually ran out of goodies for the Halloween visitors. As he continued to think of his homily, he hoped the bell would not ring again.

But it did.

Opening the door, he found a neighbor and her three-year-old daughter. "I'm sorry," he told the child, "but I don't have a single 'goodie' in my house to give you."

The child looked up at Deacon Lewis, held up her bag of treats and said, "Then you can have one of mine."

For Deacon Lewis, that night, kindness came knocking at his front door.

> **'Let the little children come to Me . . . for it is to such as these that the kingdom of God belongs.' (Mark 10:14)**

> *Loving God, open our eyes and our hearts to see You in every person.*

Day-by-everyday

The musical "Godspell" had a long and very successful run on Broadway. One of its most popular songs went something like this: "to see thee more clearly, to love thee more dearly, to follow thee more nearly, day by day."

That was an adaptation from a prayer written in the 13th century by St. Richard of Chichester. In his late 30s the educator became chancellor of Oxford University. Within a decade he was ordained a priest and elected bishop of Chichester.

Here's St. Richard's prayer:

"Thank you, Lord Jesus Christ, / For all the benefits and blessings which You have given me, / For all the pains and insults which You have borne for me. / Merciful Friend, Brother and Redeemer, / may I know You more clearly, / Love You more dearly, / And follow You more nearly, / Day by day."

A saint's prayer which, if lived, daily, today, could help make us saints.

I am the way, and the truth, and the life. No one comes to the Father except through Me. (John 14:6)

Enable me to be grateful and loyal to You, Lord Jesus Christ.

Faith's limits before "the void"

When a French archbishop called death "the void" some were shocked. Is it possible to speak of "the void" while believing in an afterlife?

Peter Steinfels in the *New York Times* reminds us of some facts of death. Death is ". . . a dissolution of all that is familiar, a sudden yank or a slow yielding into the unknown . . . a hairline crack that . . . at any instant can . . . swallow whatever was solid and certain."

Believing that dying we fall into the arms of a loving God helps. But, remember, Jesus, dying on His cross, experienced this terror, too.

And then there's "the void" between us and our Creator. Accepting that God cannot be tamed by human language or concepts is always a leap into nothingness.

To acknowledge our fear of death is not a denial of faith in life after death. Genuine faith always has its doubts. The answers await us on the far side of the mystery of death.

My God, I cry by day, but You do not answer; and by night, but find no rest. Yet . . . in You our ancestors trusted . . . You delivered them. (Psalm 22:2-3,4)

Fear and doubt do come, Redeemer. I do not ask to be delivered from them but that You walk with me through the void.

What difference does *one* vote make?

Before any election day, many say: "Why should I vote? What difference will my *one* vote make?" Well, consider these facts:

● In 1645, one vote gave Oliver Cromwell control of England.

● In 1649, one vote caused Charles I of England to be executed.

● In 1776, one vote gave America the English language instead of German.

● In 1845, one vote brought Texas into the Union.

● In 1868, one vote saved President Andrew Johnson from impeachment.

● In 1875, one vote changed France from a monarchy to a republic.

● In 1876, one vote gave Rutherford B. Hayes the presidency of the United States.

● In 1923, one vote gave Adolf Hitler the leadership of the Nazi Party.

● In 1941, one vote saved Selective Service — just weeks before Pearl Harbor was attacked.

Your vote counts — if you cast it.

We, who are many, are one body in Christ, and individually we are members one of another. (Romans 12:5)

Give me Your wisdom, Lord, to make the right choices.

A house is more than a home

The National Trust for Historic Preservation does more than just aid in the restoration of old buildings, they make dreams a reality.

They also give special awards of commendation to those who have restored and refurbished their homes. Julia Holloway Hudson and Mariam Gilbert won prizes in the Great American Home Awards' Special Category — Urban Homes.

If you go to the historic Fort Greene section of Brooklyn you will see the two award-winning restored homes, gleaming pale gray-blue-green and gray-beige-brown, their original colors. This is all made possible with the aid of the fund's staff members who shepherd owners through the legal intricacies of refinancing their mortgages at a low rate and advise them on getting the best construction help.

Mrs. Gilbert laughs, "I'll be paying off this house for the rest of my life, but I'm glad I did it. It pleases me, and it beats a tombstone."

What will be your memorial? Will it be built on God?

Unless the Lord builds the house, those who build it labor in vain. (Psalm 127:1)

Lord, come dwell in my house.

Choosing your attitude

It has been said that the one thing we humans get to choose in any and all circumstances is our attitude. Attitude can do more than change the way we feel. It can change the way we act. It can even change lives.

Henry Fawcett, a 20-year-old Englishman, joined his father on a hunting trip. In a horrendous accident, the older man's shotgun discharged. His son was blinded.

Henry Fawcett had looked forward to a bright future. Now he nearly gave in to despair. But one thing mattered more to him than blindness or bitterness, love for his father. His father was so distraught the young man feared for his sanity. So Henry Fawcett decided to pretend what he did not feel: hope for a full life.

He not only convinced his father, but himself. He took on a new interest in life. In time he was elected to Parliament and later became postmaster general. Henry Fawcett had a satisfying career and useful life because he willed himself to change his attitude.

Choose your attitude carefully.

If we hope for what we do not see, we wait for it with patience. (Romans 8:25)

Grant me wisdom in using my free will, Spirit of God.

Take five . . . or maybe ten

If you find yourself constantly wanting to "get away from it all," or if visions of tropical islands invade your thoughts, it may mean that you need a break.

While hopping on an airplane may be nice, what you're probably seeking is the reduction of stress associated with vacations. You can reduce stress everyday by increasing your leisure time with these helpful tips.

■ Learn the art of saying no. Biting off more than you can chew only leads to anxiety. Allow the feeling of stress caused by some requests to automatically trigger a polite refusal.

■ Schedule "down" time. Leave some space in your daily planner empty. When the time arrives go where your spirit moves you.

■ Try lyming. This Caribbean term means doing absolutely nothing guilt free. Dr. Harold Bloomfield, co-author of *The Power of 5,* says, "It gives your brain time to process information it's receiving when you're in overload."

Vacations are great but allow yourself to be unoccupied at some point every day.

It is in vain that you rise up early and go late to rest, eating the bread of anxious toil; for He gives sleep to His beloved. (Psalm 127:2)

Lord, remind me to slow down.

One nurse, much kindness

For someone in pain no act of kindness is small. For John Burnley, who was in the hospital to have kidney stones removed, one particular nurse proved that a little compassion means a lot.

With post-operative pain worsened by complications, he got little sleep. One night he was especially restless and ill. Just closing his eyes disoriented him. Nurse Roseanne Caruso came in to check on him and, realizing his discomfort, sat down to talk.

The nurse listened to his concerns. She adjusted the lights and blinds to make him more comfortable. Since it was not a busy night on the floor, she invited the patient to sit at the nurses' station for a while. After about an hour he was able to return to his room and sleep through the night.

In a letter he later wrote to Nurse Caruso, John Burnley said, "You made considerable time to listen to me, then suggested positive and creative solutions that were of significant benefit to my state of mind and ultimately provided me with some much needed sleep." She did "far more than I would have expected."

When you receive kindness, say "Thanks."

Do not withhold kindness. (Sirach 7:33)

Lord, bless all who show compassion.

An unbroken record

It was absolutely amazing! On November 8, 1970, history was made in Tulane Stadium under the most improbable circumstances.

The Detroit Lions and the New Orleans Saints were playing. There was no time left on the clock. The Saints were down by a score of 17-16, and the offensive coach called for the field-goal team. The goal posts were 63 yards away.

Everyone thought the coach had lost his mind. Then Tom Dempsey, 23, with a withered arm and half of his kicking foot missing, wearing a specially constructed shoe, kicked the longest field goal in NFL history, a record which still stands. And the Saints won, 19-17.

Dempsey remains indebted to his father for teaching him to deal with his disabilities and to surmount them. "He'd say, 'There's no such thing as can't. You can do anything you want to do. You just may have to do it differently from other people.'"

Every generous act of giving, with every perfect gift, is from above. (James 1:17)

Father, help me to be all that I can be, not only for myself, but for others.

Between fire and flood

Mike Maidenburg, publisher of *The Grand Forks Herald,* promised his paper would publish "come hell or high water . . . As it turned out, we got both."

The building where the North Dakota newspaper was published was destroyed in a fire that claimed much of the downtown area while flood water hindered firefighters. It was part of the devastation caused when the Red River flooded in 1997 to an extent not known in 500 years.

While issues of the paper going back over a hundred years are available on microfilm, the extensive clipping files that local people counted on for family historical records are gone. For example, a wedding story could tell "the best friend of the groom, the best friend of the bride. It lists relatives and friends, what kind of party they had."

It is hard to lose ties to the past, ties that give families roots. It is even harder to keep going, to rebuild. But the paper and the city have promised to do just that. The determination of all who face disasters should be applauded and supported.

Naomi saw that (Ruth) was determined to go with her . . . So the two of them . . . came to Bethlehem . . . Naomi returned together with Ruth the Moabite, her daughter-in-law. (Ruth 1:18,19,22)

Show me how to be helpful, caring Lord.

Doing the impossible

At some point in life everyone is called on to do more than they ever thought possible. Coping with illness. Financial problems. Loss of a loved one. Some goal you have set that others try to talk you out of pursuing.

Whatever the challenge, perseverance counts. Dealing with difficulties as well as the well-meaning but sometimes inappropriate remarks of those around you, takes effort and time. It is easy to get discouraged. It takes discipline to keep going.

U.S. Olympic champion Carl Lewis had this thought on keeping focused on what you need to do: "If you go by other people's opinions or predictions, you'll just end up talking yourself out of something. If you're running down the track of life thinking that it's impossible to break life's records, those thoughts have a funny way of sinking into your feet."

What separates the possible from the impossible in your life?

I can do all things through Him who strengthens me. (Philippians 4:13)

It is so easy to allow the opinions of others to interfere with what I need to do. Help me to listen for truly useful advice, Lord, but to keep the decision-making between You and me.

Wisdom for life

Cardinal Joseph Bernardin died in November, 1996, after suffering from pancreatic cancer. He was a much-loved priest and bishop for the Diocese of Chicago.

In his final week of life, as he faced death with grace and courage, he wrote the United States Supreme Court, asking the justices to reject arguments that the dying have a right to a physician-assisted suicide.

"As one who is dying, I have especially come to appreciate the gift of life," Bernardin wrote. "Illness draws you inside yourself. We focus on our own pain. We may feel sorry for ourselves or become depressed. But by focusing on Jesus' message — that through suffering we empty ourselves and are filled with God's grace and love — we can begin to think of other people and their needs. When we are ill, we need people the most."

Wise words from a wise man. Listen to his words — and those of Jesus — and help others in need.

Rejoice in hope, be patient in suffering, persevere in prayer. (Romans 12:12)

Merciful Savior, ease the agony of the dying.

An uncommon life

Annie Smith Peck's family did not approve of her. Born into a traditional Rhode Island family during the Victorian age, they did not expect her to attend college. She did. She was the first woman to enroll in the American School of Classical Studies in Athens.

But she really shocked them by falling in love with mountains and mountain climbing. When Annie Smith Peck saw the Alps she promised herself that she would develop the knowledge and endurance to be a climber. When she returned to climb the Matterhorn in 1895 she became world famous. She set her sights even higher by attempting peaks that challenged the best male climbers.

In 1906 she became the first American, man or woman, to climb Peru's 22,204 foot Mount Huascaran. Its north peak was named in her honor. She was 58 years old. And Annie Smith Peck kept climbing her beloved mountains until three years before her death at 85.

Only then did she return home. The inscription on her gravestone reads: "You have brought uncommon glory to women of all time."

You are the great pride of our nation! (Judith 15:9)

Lord, let us bring You glory by being the individuals You want us to be.

Struggling with words

Do you have a fear of public speaking? Many people do. One survey a few years ago found that more people were afraid of speaking in front of a group than of dying!

Even Billy Graham, considered by many to be a great speaker, admits his own apprehension. "When I start . . . I'm scared because it is a responsibility to tell people about eternal things from the Bible," Graham says. "You are actually speaking, in a sense, for God. I have a strong fear I will say something that will mislead someone. Many times I've gone up there and wished the floor would open up and let me fall through."

As the Greek philosopher Aristotle believed, "It is not enough to know what to say, it is necessary also to know how to say it."

Good communication skills are the sign of a leader. Great leaders can touch people's hearts and minds, and bring positive change to this world.

You can be a leader.

Let no one boast about human leaders. (1 Corinthians 3:21)

Teacher and Master, call many to servant leadership.

"Plant some good stuff"

Chad Everett was at the top of his acting career in the 1970's. You may remember him as Dr. Joe Gannon on TV's "Medical Center."

When the series ended, Everett found himself without a job or any acting offers. He turned to alcohol for comfort, and became an alcoholic.

One day, he asked God to take away his addiction. "From the moment I said, 'Father, take this from me,' I knew I was on my way. I had never really given anything up to God that way, that passionately," says Everett. "My spiritual garden was full of weeds until I quit drinking. I had to pull out the weeds and plant some good stuff. I was letting a bottle control my life instead of God."

Admitting that we have an addiction — whether it's alcohol, drugs, food, gambling, shopping, or something else — is the first step to healing. If you or a loved one are caught in the grip of an addiction, seek the aid of a professional. But be sure to turn to God for comfort and help.

> **Jesus said to (Bartimaeus), 'What do you want Me to do for you?' The blind man said to Him, 'My teacher, let me see again.' Jesus said to him, 'Go; your faith has made you well.' (Mark 10:51-52)**

Savior, bring us to freedom.

It's been fun

Designers talk about form and function. There are times when the marriage seems so perfect, one can hardly imagine a better design. Consider the humble bean pot.

Historically it probably derives from Roman ovoid cooking pots. Robin Bloksberg, writing in *Yankee* magazine, says the "shape is perfectly suited to . . . very slow, unattended cooking . . . The thick clay insulates against burning. The bulging belly disperses heat. And the narrowed top limits surface exposure."

Rarely marked by potters and therefore hard to date, they are rarely desired by collectors. Still, families do pass them down. And to allay fears about lead in early glazes, people can give them a home lead test just in case their heirloom is poisonous.

Traditional baked bean suppers evoke the spirit of New England even for folks far away.

Connections with the past are important. Make room in your life for an appreciation of the past. And an appreciation of simple things that are, somehow, just about perfect.

> **Your word is a lamp to my feet and a light to my path. (Psalm 119:105)**

> *God, help me look with new eyes at simple and useful things so I can value them more.*

A more noble life

The parable of the Good Samaritan is probably among the best known stories of the Bible. For 2,000 years people have heard and read the words and attempted to understand them.

Living the words is hard. Rev. Dr. Martin Luther King Jr. offered an observation that can help us answer the question, "Who is my neighbor?"

"The ultimate measure of a man is not where he stands in moments of comfort and convenience, but where he stands at times of challenge and controversy. The true neighbor will risk his position, his prestige, and even his life for the welfare of others. In dangerous valleys and hazardous pathways, he will lift some bruised and beaten brother to a higher and more noble life."

We pass by people in trouble everyday. It is too risky, too time-consuming, too much trouble to stop. But if we do stop anyway, we succeed not just in proving to "the other guy" that we are good neighbors, but we prove it to ourselves.

You do well if you really fulfill the royal law according to the scripture, 'You shall love your neighbor as yourself.' (James 2:8)

Spirit of God, help me put aside my fear and reach out my hand to my brothers and sisters in need.

Creative living, living creatively

In her book, *Women Who Run With the Wolves,* Clarissa Pinkola Estes writes that "Creativity is a shape changer. One moment it takes this form, the next that. It is like a dazzling spirit who appears to us all, yet is hard to describe for no one agrees on what they saw in that brilliant flash."

How do you live with this "brilliant flash"? Be alert to intuition. Be courageous.

Discover the not-yet-found in even common place events, things. Yours is a unique vision.

Learn to read the signs of the times, the signs of life.

Listen to stories. Savor beauty.

Allow your soul to express itself in speech, in actions, in what you write, in how you decorate your home, in the clothes you wear, in worship.

And be flexible. There are times to go with the flow, moment-by-moment.

I have filled him with divine spirit, with ability, intelligence, and knowledge in every kind of craft. (Exodus 31:3)

Thank You, Divine Artisan, for making me creative.

Free-throw fame

At age 70, Tom Amberry retired from his career as a podiatrist. That's when he took up his new hobby: shooting baskets.

He says "basketball is a universal language." It is obviously one he speaks with ease. Eighteen months after he began practicing, he sank 2,750 consecutive free-throws and earned a place in the *Guinness Book of Records*.

His teaching video has become a tool for coaches around the country and he's added a book on the subject. He keeps in practice by shooting 500 free-throws a day.

Here's Tom Amberry's secret: "Half of it is using the right mechanics. Half is psychological. Another half is practice." It is a guide he offers as seriously as he does humorously.

Knowing what to do and how to do it is part of any success story. But practicing, putting your talents and abilities to the test over and over is hard but necessary work. Add to that an element of true enjoyment and your task will be lighter.

Let us run with perseverance the race that is set before us, looking to Jesus the pioneer and perfecter of our faith. (Hebrews 12:1-2)

Help me discover things that matter to me, Holy Spirit, and help me do them with a focused mind and a happy heart.

Giving your all

Sometimes the way in which The Christopher motto, "It's better to light one candle than to curse the darkness" is put into action can be refreshing.

Lisa Wedemeyer joined the National Bone Marrow Registry. Sooner than expected she proved a match with a patient.

Despite her husband's misgivings — he's in the medical field — she signed consent forms, donated her bone marrow, and wrote a note to go with it. She knew only that the recipient was a woman.

She received a note in reply. She wrote back. And a year-long correspondence was begun. At the close of the year Lisa was given the woman's real name, Mary, and her address.

That night Mary phoned. She and Lisa talked for about 20 minutes. Exactly a week later Lisa took a phone call. Mary had died. Lisa was devastated.

But as a National Bone Marrow Registry staff member reminded her, the gift of her bone marrow had given Mary a year of life she would not otherwise have enjoyed.

I came that they may have life, and have it abundantly. (John 10:10)

Enable us, in imitation of You, Jesus, to give abundant life to others.

By the heat of the moon

Scientists recently discovered an unexpected source of warmth. The full moon raises the temperature of the earth by a fraction of a degree.

The scientists who made the discovery think the most likely cause is infrared radiation reflected from the sun.

So, although the visible light we receive from the moon is pale and cold-looking, we also receive invisible heat that warms the air.

By raising global temperatures just slightly, the moon may influence air circulation patterns and our weather.

That's a reminder that the warmth of small kindnesses can also have far-reaching effects. They can influence the direction of lives, assuage loneliness, cheer the sad.

You have made the moon to mark the seasons; the sun knows its time for setting. (Psalm 104:19)

Help us radiate Your kindness to us, Creator-God, sharing it with all we meet. Let each act of loving kindness shine brightly in a world that seems dark and cold.

Without thinking twice

Denise Terry and her husband, Michael, were out walking with their children and dog one cold winter morning in Nebraska when they saw four little boys playing on a frozen lagoon — and then saw two fall through the thin ice. One climbed out, but the other was in over his head.

Immediately the couple rushed to the rescue. Shouting to onlookers to telephone police, the couple ventured onto the ice.

Eventually — after falling in and pulling herself out twice — Denise got close enough to throw the dog's leash to the boy, telling him to wrap it around his hands. He did, and Denise pulled him out of the water. Local firemen completed the rescue.

"We didn't think twice about helping that boy," Denise says. "I just thought of him as someone else's child. I mean, if you were in that situation, what would you do?"

The Lord is the stronghold of my life; of whom shall I be afraid? (Psalm 27:1)

Give us the strength, Lord, to face the challenges of every day.

Good words not from the Good Book

Many people grow up learning verses from the Bible. Occasionally, some familiar phrases sound like they come from the Scriptures, but have a different source.

"The Lord helps those who help themselves." Those words were actually paraphrased by Ben Franklin from the writings of the ancient Greek poet Aeschylus.

"Neither a borrower nor a lender be" is advice from Shakespeare by way of his play *Hamlet*.

"Cleanliness is next to godliness" comes from evangelical preacher John Wesley, the 18th century founder of Methodism.

Words of wisdom can come from many sources. But the Bible offers more than human wisdom. It offers God's own truth and holiness.

Start a habit for yourself of spending some time every day with the Scriptures. You will find words of life to remember and to live.

All scripture is inspired by God and is useful for teaching, for reproof, for correction, and for training in righteousness, so that everyone who belongs to God may be proficient, equipped for every good work.
(2 Timothy 3:16-17)

Teach me Your knowledge, Your wisdom, Counselor.

Need a lift?

"No cover, no minimum and everybody is welcome," is how Bruce Renfroe, an elevator operator for the New York City Transit Authority, describes the subway station elevator that he's transformed into a miniature jazz club.

Originally a train cleaner, he permanently injured his knee several years ago and was placed on elevator duty as a result. Rather than let the situation bring him down, he uses it to pick people up.

In his elevator at the 181st Street station, he orchestrates a 30-second ride that is known as a peaceful oasis in a sea of rushing commuters.

Step into the elevator and you are greeted by black and white portraits, hanging plants, and the soothing sounds of the jazz that Bruce Renfroe loves so much. From the CD player in the corner, he carefully chooses the musical selections that have become the daily delight of so many.

He says, "There's a lot of stress out there, and all I try to do is get everybody in a mellow mood."

Share something you love with the people you work with and everyone will enjoy coming to work a little bit more.

God loves a cheerful giver.
(2 Corinthians 9:7)

Lord, may we bring You to our workplaces.

A meal and a hug

An older woman stopped in a small-town cafe to have lunch. A younger woman, seated with her small boy, invited the newcomer to join her and her son. So the older woman sat down with them.

The younger woman told her new friend that she was married with five children but that this child, Eric, was "very precious to us for we almost lost him." "He was born prematurely and has had multiple health problems," the young mother said. She added that during the many times she spent at a medical center she often ate alone. And that's when she made up her mind to invite anyone she saw eating alone to join her.

After they finished their meal, the two women said good-bye. For his farewell, Eric hugged his mother's new friend.

Our own life experiences — especially our times of sorrow, loneliness, suffering — can teach us to treat others with greater compassion and kindness.

He had to become like His brothers and sisters in every respect, so that He might be a merciful and faithful high priest in the service of God, to make a sacrifice of atonement for the sins of the people. (Hebrews 2:17)

Help us to learn empathy from our experiences, Lord.

For all and everything, thanks!

After you think about your reasons for gratitude, you might breathe a thanksgiving prayer like this:

"For the sparkle in the eyes of loved ones / for the touch of a friendly hand / for the bread we eat / for the plentiful stars / for the roar of the breakers /

"For the Holy Word You have spoken to us . . . / for the chance to be / and to do / we thank You / O Lord, our God. / Amen."

Thank those who have given you the gift of life.

Thank those who have given you their love, concern, time, talents and self.

Thank earth's creatures for the gift of their fierceness, beauty, unique intelligence, companionship.

And thank the Earth, our unique home.

All is a gift. Gratitude is the only response.

With gratitude in your hearts sing psalms, hymns, and spiritual songs to God . . . giving thanks to God the Father through (Jesus). (Colossians 3:16,17)

For You, Your love, thank You, generous God.

Talking turkey

What do we know about the first Thanksgiving?

Well, we know that this feast was held in 1621 to mark the Pilgrims' first harvest. We know, too, that the meal was eaten outdoors, that Native Americans and Pilgrims dined together, and that turkey and pumpkin found their way to the table.

The most important fact we know about the fall feast has little to do with guests or food; it is a fact about feeling. Wrote Edward Winslow, a partaker of that meal: ". . . by the goodness of God, we are so far from want that we often wish you partakers of our plenty."

Although the Pilgrims did not celebrate this feast each year, we can be fairly certain that often throughout the years that followed they took stock of their lives, thanking God for His goodness in offering them plenty — and praying that His bounty be given to those especially in need.

> **O give thanks to the Lord, for He is good, for His steadfast love endures forever. . . . Who rescued us from our foes . . . Who gives food to all flesh, for His steadfast love endures forever. (Psalm 136:1,24,25)**

> *Unite all citizens of every race and creed in one hymn of thanksgiving to You, sustaining Lord.*

No time for silent nights

During the Christmas season, while others may think of time off from work, priests and ministers must work overtime.

"The day after Thanksgiving, I checked my schedule and realized I had five free nights between then and Christmas," said Rev. Arthur Caliandro, pastor of New York's Marble Collegiate Church.

At Calvary Church in Grand Rapids, Michigan, Rev. Ed Dobson said the "result is exhaustion."

Rev. Timothy Power, pastor of Pax Christi Catholic Church in a Minneapolis suburb, is the only resident priest in a parish expecting about 12,000 people at seven Christmas Eve/Christmas Day Masses. A visiting priest and parishioners help.

Despite the stress and strain, many clergy enjoy the season and the opportunities it brings to reach people spiritually. Said one, "It provides a wonderful opportunity for precisely what we've been called to do."

> **For this gospel I was appointed a herald and an apostle and a teacher, and for this reason I suffer . . . But I . . . know the One in whom I . . . trust. (2 Timothy 1:11-12)**

> *God, give me the strength to go on even when I'm too weary.*

Case solved: Clue's creator found

Professor Plum. Mrs. Peacock. Colonel Mustard. Miss Scarlett.

You might know these famous participants in the popular board game Clue. But you probably don't have a clue as to who created the game, known in Britain as Cluedo.

The following might help solve the mystery. Waddington's, the company that first published the game in 1948, went on a hunt for its creator, Anthony E. Pratt, to have him join ceremonies planned to mark the 150-millionth worldwide sale of the game. At the time, the company didn't know Mr. Pratt had died in 1994.

Mr. Pratt, a British law clerk, came up with the idea for a board version of a popular parlor game while walking the beat as a fire warden during World War II. His wife helped design the game's nine-room house.

The inventor of this murder mystery died peacefully in a nursing home, reportedly of natural causes.

Don't wait to honor and thank those who deserve it.

An intelligent mind acquires knowledge, and the ear of the wise seeks knowledge. (Proverbs 18:15)

Give us understanding, Lord, as we try to fathom some of life's mysteries.

Words of gratitude

Not much is known about the English mystic Julian of Norwich, including her real name. She lived as a hermit. Her *Revelations of Divine Love* told of her visions of the Passion of Christ and of the Holy Trinity.

Her words still touch many today. Here she offers a most intimate and loving prayer of thanksgiving:

> "O God,
> as truly as You are our Father,
> so just as truly are You our Mother.
> We thank You God, our Father,
> for Your strength and goodness.
> We thank You God, our Mother,
> for the closeness of Your caring.
> O God, our loving Parent,
> we thank You for the great love
> You have for each one of us. Amen."

I will give thanks to the Lord with my whole heart; I will tell of all Your wonderful deeds. I will be glad and exult in You; I will sing praise to Your name, O Most High. (Psalm 9:1-2)

Thank You, today, loving God. Thank You, yesterday, gentle God. Thank You, tomorrow, compassionate God.

A song to God

We are familiar with hymns and prayers of praise to God from Christian and Jewish traditions and other modern religions. But here is one from Epictetus, a Greek Stoic philosopher of the second century, A.D. He believed in the importance of self-control and the acceptance of the natural order, which is itself the will of God. His prayer still has meaning:

"What else can I do, a lame old man,
but sing hymns to God?
If I were a nightingale, I would do the
nightingale's part.
If I were a swan, I would do as a swan.
But now I am a rational creature,
and I ought to praise God:
this is my work;
I do it, nor will I desert my post,
so long as I am allowed to keep it.
And I exhort you to join me in the same
song."

Let the children of Zion rejoice in their King. Let them praise His name with dancing, making melody to Him with tambourine and lyre. (Psalm 149:2-3)

Let me live the full human life You planned for me, my God, with joy and wisdom and with constant praise for You.

Knitting to create and soothe

Knitting is neither old-fashioned nor out of fashion these days.

Some are coming back to the craft. Others are learning for the first time. And the hobby is catching on with younger people and professionals. Enthusiasts include Joanne Woodward and Steve Allen.

Melanie Falick, author of *Knitting in America,* believes that "we live in such a frenetic world, and knitting is very far away from all that. It appeals to the creative instinct, which is being ignored."

For some, knitting has gone high-tech. Knitting machines have been around for years. But they have gotten more and more sophisticated. Now people can even input designs into computers, attach it to their knitting machines and see the item appear. Human beings are still needed to cast stiches on and off, shaping the piece.

Still what most knitters want is what most of us seek: an opportunity to be creative, to relax, and to make something worthwhile.

Teach me Your way, O Lord . . . give me an undivided heart to revere Your name. (Psalm 86:11)

My hands and my heart can do so much good. Guide me, gentle God, in putting them at Your service.

Designed by and for elders

In the winter of 1986 three Lakota Sioux elders froze to death in their homes on the Pine Ridge Reservation in South Dakota. When photographer Gail Russell found out she decided to act.

She got seven friends together, all Lakota grandmothers, to come up with a plan. What they put together was an Adopt A Grandparent Program to help elders and their families in times of need.

The project converts donations from "grandchildren" into certificates for food and electricity, and fuels like propane and wood. Clothes and household items are sent directly to the recipient. Adopt A Grandparent has now spread to other areas.

Many of those who support the program are themselves American Indians who were adopted out of their tribes. It gives them a sense of belonging.

It is human to need to belong and to need to contribute. Ask yourself how you can combine these to satisfy yourself and those who could use a helping hand.

Rich experience is the crown of the aged. (Proverbs 25:6)

Elders have so much to give, Blessed Trinity. Show us how to take from them and how to give.

In the spirit's ice age

We think of Scandinavia as bitterly cold. But except in remote northern areas, it isn't as cold as the north central United States. In Stockholm, the average January temperature is 27 degrees. In Minneapolis, the average is 12 degrees.

But there is still reason to regard Scandinavia as the land of ice. True, the temperature in most Scandinavian cities is not extremely low. But it *stays* a few degrees below freezing throughout the long winter, so the ice rarely thaws.

We can have similar situations in our lives. Long, unbroken stretches of illness or other problems can be more discouraging than worse problems of shorter duration.

During such times, we can keep up our spirits by trusting God to get us through our soul's icebound winter.

I cry to You, O Lord; I say, "You are my refuge, my portion in the land of the living." Give heed to my cry for I am brought very low. (Psalm 142:5-6)

You have been my God from the first moment of my existence. You brought me alive into this world. You've kept me in Your faithful loving care to this very moment. Enable me to always trust in Your love, Your care.

Art for all ages

Third graders at Charles R. Bugg Elementary in Raleigh, N.C., study with a writer-in-residence and learn how to choreograph a dance to go with their original poems. The Ashley River Creative Arts Elementary School in Charleston, South Carolina, is devoted to arts and music education. Students at PS 314 in Brooklyn, New York, visit the Metropolitan Opera to see dress rehearsals. Then they use the performances to learn about subjects like history and literature.

Though many schools have been quick to drop arts programs to save money, the results at the schools mentioned above speak for themselves. Jim Fatata, principal of Bugg Elementary, says, "Attendance is up and behavior problems are down." Ashley River Elementary ranks high above the state average in standardized testing. Since PS 314 installed its program, test scores have improved enough to remove it from the state's list of worst-performing schools.

God has blessed some people with the talent to create. Children and adults should enjoy the works of art available everywhere.

(God) gave skill to human beings that He might be glorified in His marvelous works. (Sirach 38:6)

Help us appreciate the arts and artists, Lord.

The real Santa Claus

Juana Orellan Watson never forgot her disappointment when she heard from a teacher that Santa Claus only visited children in rich families. An 8-year-old living in Calnali, a remote village in Mexico, Juana vowed that one day Santa Claus would stop there.

She left Mexico, eventually settled in Indiana with her husband and three children, and developed a successful catering business. Still, the image of her village, along with her grandfather's words that it wouldn't be enough to apologize to God for not making a difference, gnawed at her.

Working with T.I.M.E. for Christ, Inc., a nondenominational medical mission group based in San Antonio, Texas, Juana Orellan Watson has made a difference and brought something better than Santa Claus to her village. They transformed Calnali's school into a medical clinic. For people who had never seen a doctor or dentist in their lifetimes, one woman's childhood promise was the most valuable gift they could ever have received.

Each of us, in our way, can make a difference.

The good leave an inheritance to their children's children. (Proverbs 13:22)

Life is a gift, Lord God. Let me give of mine freely.

Keeping the Sabbath

Is the Sabbath still a special day?

We know the traditions. Christians celebrate Sunday as the Sabbath; Jews, Saturday; Muslims, Friday. Genesis speaks of God resting from His labors of creation on the seventh day. Sabbath comes from the Hebrew word for rest.

Rabbi Abraham Joshua Heschel offered this perspective on the solemnity of the Sabbath day: "This is the task of men: to conquer space and sanctify time. All week long we are called upon to sanctify life through employing things of space. On the Sabbath it is given to us to share in the holiness that is the heart of time . . . The clean, silent rest of the Sabbath leads us to a realm of endless peace, or to the beginning of an awareness of what eternity means."

Celebrate your faith's Sabbath. It is indeed the day of the Lord.

> **Refrain from trampling the sabbath, from pursuing your own interests on My holy day. (Isaiah 58:13)**

> *Show us Yourself, Holy God, every day of the week. But grant us the privilege of enjoying the Sabbath with You in a special and holy way.*

It's a mind game

When you think of the words "students" and "competition," do you immediately think of sports?

The fact is, academic competitions are on the rise. Many use sports vocabulary such as leagues, tournaments and teams, but they are all about knowledge. Some serious competitors study up to 40 hours a week for major events. The prize is not just prestige, but scholarship money, sometimes thousands of dollars. Contests range from We the People — on knowledge of the Constitution — to the National Spelling Bee to the U.S. Academic Decathalon and many others.

Some people criticize competitions, saying they are counter to real education. But one teacher says that while "we still look at athletics as a game, . . . succeeding in school is about the core of what an acceptable person is in our society."

Learning should still be the most important thing. But if the pressure on students outweighs the fun, something is wrong.

(Wisdom) will find him with the bread of learning, and give him the water of wisdom to drink. (Sirach 15:3)

Lord, inspire me to give my best, but always using common sense to determine the right balance for my life.

Rich man — in money and love

Richard Paul Evans' first novel, *The Christmas Box,* became a bestseller and made him a rich man. Not content to spend the money solely on himself and his family, the 33-year-old established a philanthropic organization to help out others as well.

His book, also made into a TV movie, deals with lessons learned within a family where a child has died. The story touched the hearts of many people, especially grieving parents.

"People say 'thank you' to me and I don't totally understand," Mr. Evans says. "But I'm moved by their pain."

Mr. Evans' parents feel enriched by helping their son run the Christmas Box foundation. Mr. Evans says his mother's experience of having had a stillborn baby when he was a child inspired his book. Back then, she says, she couldn't fully mourn her loss. But "now I'm helping other women who have suffered."

Those who are generous are blessed. (Proverbs 22:9)

Inspire me, Lord, to share the gifts and talents I have with others.

Weddings that work

Engaged to be married? Planning for your big day?

Here are some suggestions from "The God Squad," Rev. Tom Hartman and Rabbi Marc Gellman, for prolonging and enhancing the celebration.

Put what you love about your spouse-to-be in a letter. Then, after you have exchanged rings and are still holding hands, have the priest, minister or rabbi read at least excerpts from those letters.

Rewrite the wedding vows to answer this question: "Why do I want to commit to my spouse for better or for worse, for richer, for poorer, in sickness and in health?"

Include prayers of thanksgiving for significant departed family members in the ceremony. Pray for living elderly family members, too.

Ask family and friends to participate in the wedding service as readers, best man, maid or matron of honor.

Don't forget the poor and needy. Have guests bring a basket of food for a needy family, or a charitable donation to the wedding ceremony.

Little children, let us love, not in word or speech, but in truth and action. (1 John 3:18)

Bless engaged and newly married couples, Jesus.

Adopt-a-nun

Sister Mary Rinaldi is Development Director for the Salesian Sisters of St. John Bosco based in North Haledon, New Jersey. She realized that bake and garage sales could not raise the increasingly large capital needed to care for the order's aging population. So she developed a unique fund-raising program.

Here's the way it works. A person can "adopt" a nun with a $100 a year donation. In return, the nuns become special spiritual advocates for the donors. They also correspond with each other.

The original idea came from a man whose brother had been raised by nuns after being separated from his family in Italy during World War II.

Sister Mary Rinaldi says it has given the older nuns "a new feeling of being wanted, of being needed, that they still have a job to do. And what are they best at but prayer?"

They began their journey for the sake of Christ . . . Therefore we ought to support such people, so that we may become coworkers with the truth. (3 John 7,8)

Give comfort, O Lord, to those who serve You and Your people.

Making a difference by caring

It's good to hear about a company president who cares about more than profits.

Aaron Feuerstein cares about people.

Feuerstein's textile factory in Massachusetts employed 3,200 people at generous wages. When the factory was destroyed by fire, employees feared it wouldn't be rebuilt. After all, Feuerstein was 70 years old.

But Feuerstein announced that he would rebuild. He would also continue paying employees' wages and benefits for at least a month. Then he extended this arrangement, and began rebuilding as fast as possible.

He said, "There's somebody out there who's not working if I don't come through."

One caring person is making a real difference.

You shall not withhold the wages of poor and needy laborers. (Deuteronomy 24:14)

Inspire employers to pay equal wages for equal work, Harvest Master.

Contending with the holiday blues

Holiday depression afflicts millions.

Christmas, for instance, can become more a reminder of loss and aloneness than the opportunity to focus on and celebrate the birth of Jesus.

Experts say one of the first essentials in dealing with the holiday blues is to acknowledge your feelings. Living with the loss of a loved one is especially painful. One grief counselor says, "If you feel like crying, cry; if you feel like laughing, laugh. Grief is very personal." Accepting that a holiday will not be what it once was is important.

Other ways to contend with the holiday blahs? Volunteer at a soup kitchen, dine with a friend, drive to the beach or the mountains, or spend the day with God.

In the end, loss reveals truths to us. And the Spirit is with us throughout.

Abide in Me as I abide in you. (John 15:4)

You who faced the agonies and tragedies of life, be with me this day.

Neighborly love

Philadelphians proved to one of their neighbors that they truly live in the "city of brotherly love."

The *Philadelphia Daily News* featured the story of Joyce Gordon Moody, a woman who had crack addicts living next door. The addicts had been getting high and drunk. One day they robbed her house, pointed a gun at her, smashed her car windshield and slashed the tires. She and her 11-year-old son were terrified of leaving the house. That threatened to ruin their Christmas.

Readers of the *Daily News* helped. People came to her house with food and gifts. A lawyer volunteered his services. A glass company installed a new windshield. A New Jersey family brought gifts for her son, Lemar. The Deputy Police Commissioner promised whatever help the department could legally do.

It was a joyous Christmas. "My boy was the happiest boy," Moody said. "It was so uplifting to know that people cared. I will never forget what so many people did for me."

Lift someone's heart this Christmas and every day.

You have pain now; but I will see you again, and your hearts will rejoice. (John 16:22)

Holy Spirit, inspire us to help our neighbors.

"A great miracle happened there"

The year was 165 B.C. The 24th day of the month *Kislev* in the Hebrew calendar. The place, Jerusalem. Judas Maccabeus, his brothers and their army had defeated King Antiochus and the Syrian-Greeks who had prohibited the worship of the one God and had profaned the Temple. The Temple had been cleaned and was ready for rededication. The Torah returned to its tabernacle.

But only a one day supply of olive oil for the perpetual flame before the tabernacle could be found. It burned for eight days!

The miracle has been remembered since for the eight days of Hanukkah. An eight-candled menorah is lighted, one candle a day. Latke, potato pancakes, or jelly donuts are eaten. Children receive sweets. Sometimes 18 pennies in a small hand-made fabric bag are given because the Hebrew word for eighteen is *chaim*, life. A four-sided Dreidle or top is used for games. Joy abounds.

Indeed, what is sweeter, more life-giving and a cause for rejoicing than a fierce fidelity to one's God?

Every year . . . the days of dedication of the altar should be observed with joy and gladness. (1 Maccabees 4:59)

May we be as fierce and as joyous in our fidelity to You, God, as were the Maccabees.

Falling in love

How sure must we be before making a lifetime commitment to another person?

To Jim Collins it seemed too good to be true. He was falling in love with Kristen, a woman whom he'd met only three months earlier in a city 3,000 miles away. She shared his feelings. But both were unsettled by the speed at which their relationship was moving.

Telling his story in *Yankee* magazine, Jim wrote that he was known among friends as being cautious and old-fashioned. Not a risk-taker. He said Kristen was an independent and strong-willed woman who never felt sure about her relationships.

In December, while visiting a friend's cabin in New Hampshire, the couple made a decision. "We hugged beneath the mistletoe and held on . . . I asked Kristen to marry me, the world shifting all around us, and she said yes."

Sometimes caution is called for. Other times, we need to overcome our fears and take a risk.

Be strong and very courageous. (Joshua 1:7)

Show us how to be prudent risk takers, God.

Encyclopedia to reckon with

Students and others routinely reach for a volume from one of numerous encyclopedias available on library shelves. From one volume desk versions to multi-volume sets, we find information about people and nature, places and events, science and art — the range of human knowledge — arranged by alphabet or subject for easy use.

The earliest surviving encyclopedia is Pliny the Elder's 37 volume *Natural History* from the 1st century A.D. The 1700's was a golden age for encyclopedias: Ephraim Chambers and Denis Diderot achieved fame and the first edition of the *Encyclopedia Britannica* appeared.

But no encyclopedia competes with the *Yung Lo Ta Tien* for sheer size. China's first and largest encyclopedia, it was published in 11,095 books in 1408. Three thousand scholars and assistants took six years to hand-script it on rice paper. Within 300 years it was destroyed. Its only duplicate was nearly obliterated during the Boxer Rebellion with just a few hundred volumes surviving.

The human mind is capable of tremendous accomplishments. Add your contribution.

The mind of the righteous ponders how to answer. (Proverbs 15:28)

Holy Spirit, guide us in using our minds to serve Your people.

A role model in women's basketball

Do athletes owe any obligation to peers and fans? Once they've achieved personal goals must they do more?

Stanford University-educated Jennifer Azzi, 28, was a star player in Europe and helped lead the U.S. women's basketball team to a gold medal in the 1996 Olympics. She could rest on her laurels. Instead she feels a responsibility to the future of the sport and to young athletes who will follow her.

"It's great to see the progress women's basketball has made," says Ms. Azzi, a founding member of the American Basketball League. "A lot of other women fought for things that have helped us get to where we are now. I want to see it continue."

Ms. Azzi recognizes she is a role model and says, "Little girls really lack confidence and athletics build a certain confidence within." In an era when boasting is common in sports, her attitude is refreshing.

In Christ Jesus . . . we have access to God in boldness and confidence. (Ephesians 3:11,12)

Keep us alert, Lord, to the importance of constructive competition.

Sing out: Peace on earth

One of the joys of the Christmas season is the wonderful music. Many carols which are rarely heard at other times of the year have a meaning that goes beyond nostalgia or simple sentiment.

"I Heard the Bells on Christmas Day" tells of the angels' cry on that first Christmas night answering the hopelessness of our own times. Listen again to the words of Henry Wadsworth Longfellow.

> "In my despair I bowed my head.
> 'There is no peace on earth,' I said.
> For hate is strong and mocks the song
> of 'peace on earth, goodwill to men.'
> Then pealed the bells more loud and deep.
> God is not dead, nor does He sleep.
> The wrong shall fail, the right prevail
> With peace on earth, goodwill to men."

Peace to you. Peace to us all.

Praise Him with trumpet sound; praise Him with lute and harp! Praise Him with tambourine and dance; praise Him with strings and pipe! Praise Him with clanging cymbals. (Psalm 150:3-5)

Thank You, Father, Son and Holy Spirit, for the words and music and art and all things that praise You and enrich us.

For our children

Susan Brotchie of Peabody, Massachusetts, was four months pregnant when the father of her unborn child walked out. It took her nine years and endless legal battles to collect child support for her daughter, Katie.

She decided to use this incident to help others, and founded Advocates for Better Child Support (ABCS). The organization has helped over 9,000 people establish child support or collect overdue payments. While raising Katie and holding a full-time job, Susan Brotchie worked to pass laws that make collection easier.

ABCS has now opened offices in 11 states, all funded by grants and run by volunteers, and she plans to expand nationwide. "I'm trying to prevent other women from having the same experience I did," Susan Brotchie says.

People who make this world better for mothers, women, children are making the world better for the future.

As a mother comforts her child, so I will comfort you. (Isaiah 66:13)

Bless those who strive to make this a better world for all Your children, Heavenly Creator.

Glory to God

Herman Cain is the CEO and co-owner of Godfather's Pizza. He made his way to the top by working hard. But he doesn't measure his success just by the job that he holds.

"One of the keys to success in business is being happy with what you are doing, no matter what you earn," says Cain. "And give God the glory. Throughout my life, I've looked to God for guidance, but he doesn't speak through a letter or a telephone. Your spirit has to be open to his voice. He has often guided me through my wife, my mother, my children, my friends, experiences, or a Sunday morning sermon."

At times it may feel like we are praying to God for guidance, but not hearing an answer. But He is always with you. If you seek and find Him, in yourself and others, you will become an instrument of God's love.

Seek the Lord and live. (Amos 5:6)

Give us the courage to seek You, Mighty Lord.

Learn listening for life

Listening is an art form and a necessity.

Art form because listening can be both taught and learned. Necessity because active interested listening makes us genuinely human and truly spiritual.

Here's part of a Christopher "Prayer to be a Better Listener":

Teach us to listen as Your Son listened
to everyone who spoke with Him.
Remind us that, somehow, You are trying
to reach us through our partner
in conversation.
Your truth, Your love, Your goodness are
seeking us out in the truth, love and goodness
being communicated . . .
Teach us to be still, Lord
that we may truly hear our brothers and sisters
— and in them, You.

Amen.

Let everyone be quick to listen, slow to speak, slow to anger. (James 1:19)

Teach me how to listen to everyone, to every Creature, to Creation, especially to You, Dearest Lord.

Luxury in the deep freeze

Early each winter in Jukkasjarvi, Sweden, workers rebuild the village's best-known hotel. That's because the Ice Hotel melts every spring.

Carved entirely out of ice — with the exception of its wooden sauna — it attracts and amazes visitors to the Arctic. From its restaurant where reindeer meat is the specialty to its 45-foot-long bar, from the art gallery to the movie theater and the chapel, ice is everywhere and everything. Queen-sized ice beds are covered with reindeer skins and guests are given state-of-the-art sleeping bags.

A warm haven lies outside where there are heated cabins for guests who can't take the indoor temperatures of 27 to 45 degrees. Departing guests even receive survival certificates.

Most achievements of substance take a lot more endurance and persistence than one icy night. And they are worth more, too.

Endurance produces character, and character produces hope, and hope does not disappoint us, because God's love has been poured into our hearts through the Holy Spirit that has been given to us. (Romans 5:4-5)

Caring Father, I appreciate the warm comfort of Your love. Grant me the determination and strength to join my will to Yours.

Dear God, send me a socket wrench!

Stories of answered prayers are always intriguing. Here is one, told by Wayne Vanderpoel in *Guideposts*.

It all began for him in 1982 when he accompanied his pastor to a migrant camp in Florida where there is always need. Wayne was doing more than he thought he could do, when the pastor asked him to find blankets for 60 migrants. The temperature was dropping to 18 degrees, it was Christmas Day, the supplies were exhausted.

Wayne and his wife prayed and asked the local country music radio station to request blankets. A plea went out over the radio. Dozens of people brought them to his house. They had so many they couldn't fit them into the church van unless they removed all the seats. He needed an eleven-sixteenths-inch socket wrench. He had none. He prayed. A woman showed up with the wrench.

Sounds impossible? Nothing is impossible with God . . . and people who do His will.

I tell you, whatever you ask for in prayer, believe that you have received it, and it will be yours. (Mark 11:24)

Jesus, erase all doubt from my heart. Fill me with trust in Your word.

How still we see Thee lie

It was Christmas Eve, 1865, when Phillips Brooks, rector of Trinity Church, Boston, made his pilgrimage to Bethlehem. His soul was sore from America's recent Civil War, and he was in search of the consolation given by visiting the holy places of the Bible.

He sat on horseback and tried to imagine the miracle of a baby's birth 2,000 years before. He watched the night sky darken, the shepherds herding their flocks home, the emergence of brilliant stars. He got an idea.

Two years later, he shared his inspiration from the pulpit of his church. It was to be a one-time sermon, but soon there were composers who wanted to put it to music. The best known version features music by his own church organist who "dreamed" the melody.

Words by Phillips Brooks, music by Lewis H. Redner, "O Little Town of Bethlehem," we still sing of you.

Joseph also went from the town of Nazareth in Galilee to Judea, to the city of David called Bethlehem. . . . with Mary, to whom he was engaged and who was expecting a child. (Luke 2:4,5)

Keep my soul ever watchful for Your inspiration, Wisdom of God most High.

From despair to hope

Nowadays performances of Handel's *Messiah* excite audiences worldwide.

It's surprising to learn that before writing his masterpiece, George Frederick Handel was in hopeless despair. Once famous and highly praised throughout Europe, he was bankrupt and beset with misfortune that winter of 1741.

Then Handel was given the text by librettist Charles Jennens. He read it with great reluctance: "For unto us a Child is born . . . His name shall be called Wonderful Counselor, The Mighty God. . . . He was despised and rejected of men . . . But thou didst not leave His soul in hell . . . I know that my Redeemer liveth . . . King of Kings, and Lord of Lords, Hallelujah!"

As Handel read, his despair lifted. Inspired by the words, he spent two weeks at his piano refusing food and sleep while he composed the *Messiah* with its glorious Hallelujah Chorus. His composition has been a rousing success ever since.

The Lord God . . . will gather the lambs in His arms and carry them in His bosom, and gently lead the mother sheep. (Isaiah 40:10,11)

Lord, let us know Your presence in moments of despair. And grant us Your peace.

Way of peace

Dorothy Day was born in 1897. She trained as a nurse, but turned to journalism. Before her death in 1980 she had gained renown as the co-founder of the *Catholic Worker.* More than a newspaper, it is a movement to serve the poor through houses of hospitality.

She was also a peace activist, believing that peace, more than simply a lack of violence, is life-giving and positive. Peace meant not just opposition to war and personal violence, but bringing one's deepest beliefs to life everyday.

Dorothy Day said: "Paperwork, cleaning the house, cooking the meals, dealing with innumerable visitors who come all through the day, answering the phone, keeping patience and acting intelligently, which is to find some meaning in all those encounters — these . . . are the works of peace, and often seem like a very little way."

Live each day as a work of peace. It will transform you and serve those around you.

Be at peace among yourselves . . . encourage the faint hearted, help the weak, be patient. . . . See that none of you repays evil for evil. (1 Thessalonians 5:13,14,15)

Prince of Peace, let others see You in me with each word I speak and action I take.

Kitchen serves up hope

Central Kitchen in Washington, D.C., feeds the hungry in more ways than one. Besides hot meals and job training, it serves up hope.

"It's not enough to just hand food out anymore," said Robert Egger, director of the nonprofit kitchen. His staff and guest chefs run a three-month training program in kitchen arts. Annually, 48 homeless men and women acquire the basic skills necessary to begin a restaurant career.

According to one of the gourmet chef-instructors, her students here are "just as motivated to learn, and the problems of reading skills, recovering addiction and the rest were the same I faced among the middle class in the fancy school."

One 28-year-old trainee, progressing with his drug rehabilitation, initially wasn't certain he wanted to get involved. But those he met "got me to open up to my classmates, and now I really want in."

A taste of a promising future can prove irresistible.

> **Just as you did it to one of the least of these who are members of My family, you did it to Me. (Matthew 25:40)**

> *Remind us that nourishment is necessary for body, mind and soul, Jesus.*

In just an instant

Edwin Land invented Polaroid, an inexpensive and adaptable way to polarize light, in the 1930's. He set up a company to manufacture scientific instruments and anti-glare sunglasses using his process.

But it was in 1943 that his little daughter asked a question that would link his name to cameras and photo development. She simply wanted to know why she had to wait so long to see a picture he had just taken. Was there a way to make instant photographs?

He thought about it for about an hour and came up with an idea that he would spend the next four years researching. The result: the Polaroid Land Camera. It produced a finished black and white print in just 60 seconds.

There were some early glitches. The pictures started to fade after about six months. But they found an answer. And, in time, Land's colleague Howard Rogers, came up with instant color pictures. The camera was a success.

Patience is a virtue. Sometimes, impatience can be one as well, if we put it to good use.

The fruit of the Spirit is love, joy, peace, patience. (Galatians 5:22)

Guide me in serving You, God.

Housekeeper is a star

MaDonna Hossler is a remarkable woman and an equally remarkable worker by any standards.

As head housekeeper at the Kendallville, Indiana, Day's Inn, her standards are high: 20 minutes to clean a room from top to bottom, even polishing the bathroom pipes. She and her staff of 14 have been responsible for perfect quality-assurance scores on unscheduled inspections. So it was no surprise that the company named her housekeeper of the year.

The trade journal *Lodging Hospitality* got hundreds of nominations for the title of nation's best housekeeper. Some came from five-star hotels. MaDonna Hossler won again.

She does more than clean. She has been known to make home-cooked meals for regular customers on her day off. And even play a practical joke or two on them. Manager Rainelle Silver says, "The guests love her. They send her Christmas cards and everything."

Her philosophy: "I like to clean, and I love people more than anything." Loving people always shows.

Clothe yourself with humility. (1 Peter 5:5)

Help me put my whole self into my work, Lord.

Itchy ears

In a letter to a friend, St. Jerome offered the following advice about listening to gossip.

"No one wants to speak to an unwilling listener. An arrow never lodges in a stone; often it springs back and wounds the one who shot it. Let the gossip learn from your unwillingness to listen to be less ready to hurt others."

These words challenge the misperception that gossip really doesn't hurt anyone and that it can be listened to innocently. In reality, it shows an interest in matters that can be potentially embarrassing or damaging to another person. By listening we become willing accomplices.

Tuning out gossip really helps everyone involved. It protects the dignity and privacy of the person being spoken of. It protects our own dignity because we won't repeat what we don't hear. It may even teach prudence to the speaker who might be less likely to gossip about others, including you.

Gossip is defined as idle talk or rumor. Let's not engage in what is useless.

A gossip goes about telling secrets, but one who is trustworthy in spirit keeps a confidence. (Proverbs 11:13)

Gentle Teacher, show us how to treat others as we would be treated.

Ringing in the new

What would really be *new* to do on New Year's Eve? Here are some suggestions:

● *Celebrate your blessings.* Spread a table with photos, ticket stubs, greeting cards and other items that remind you of the past year's best times.

● *Write a letter.* What can you say by way of encouragement, congratulations, apology, appreciation? Send the letter to family members, friends — even yourself.

● *Forgive yourself.* Make a list of your failings during the past year. Present them to God and ask forgiveness.

● *Make a dream collage.* Cut out objects you want to buy, or choose scenes that represent how you want to feel in the coming year; paste these images on cardboard.

● *Give yourself a spiritual check-up.* Arrange to be part of a retreat at your church in the new year, or simply get together with family and friends for an afternoon of sharing the place of God in your lives.

I am the Lord your God, the Holy One of Israel, your Savior. I give Egypt as your ransom, Ethiopia and Seba in exchange for you. Because you are precious in My sight, and honored, and I love you. (Isaiah 43:3-4)

Father and Friend, every day of every year, I ask You to surround me with Your infinite love.

Also Available

If you have enjoyed this book, here are brief descriptions of other Christopher material.

● **VIDEOCASSETTES.** Our Videocassette Library ranges from wholesome entertainment to serious discussions on family life, current social issues, spiritual growth, etc.

● **APPOINTMENT CALENDAR** and **MONTHLY PLANNER.** The calendar is suitable for wall or desktop and offers an inspirational message for each day of the year. The Monthly Planner, with its slim, practical design, is handy for pocket or purse.

● **NEWS NOTES.** Published ten times a year. Many titles are available on a variety of educational, inspirational topics. Bulk and standing orders accepted. Single copies are free.

● **ECOS CRISTÓFOROS.** Spanish translations of popular News Notes. Issued 6 times a year. Single copies are free; bulk and standing orders on request.

**For more information on The Christophers
or to receive News Notes, Ecos Cristoforos or
fulfillment brochures write:
THE CHRISTOPHERS, 12 East 48th Street,
New York, NY 10017. Or phone: 212-759-4050.**